WELCOME

Andrew Francis
Chairman
Bournemouth Tourism Management Board

As the Chairman of the Bournemouth Tourism Management Board (BTMB), I am exceptionally proud of the Air Festival's success.

Now in its seventh year, the event has gone from strength to strength with attractions on the ground, in the air, at sea and the evening, making the event so much more than just an air show. Credit must be given to the continued hard work, tireless efforts and commitment of everyone involved who make the Festival the internationally renowned event it is today. I would like to take this opportunity to thank this year's partner sponsors CityFibre and Mouchel, Night Air sponsor Corona and partner Wave105 as well as all our commercial and Council partners for their support and contributions: BBC Radio Solent, BH Live, Bournemouth Airport, Campbell Rowley, Daily Echo, Bournemouth Highcliff Marriott Hotel, Hotel Miramar, Littledown Centre, Merley House, Morgan Sindall, Shepherd Neame, Stephen Young Lord of Westbury, The Cumberland Hotel, The Queens Hotel, Vulcan To The Sky Team Bournemouth and John Green of Hot Rocks for once again supplying the wristbands in support of the Air Festival charities.

I must also thank our Air Festival Patrons for their incredible support, a massive thanks to our Armed Forces; The Royal Navy, Royal Air Force, Army and Royal Marines, whose support and participation make the entire event possible. And finally a special mention and thanks to Commander Tom Herman who retires this year and has overseen Royal Navy Logistics at the festival since 2008.

Councillor Chris Mayne
The Worshipful Mayor
of Bournemouth

It is with great pleasure I welcome you to the seventh Bournemouth Air Festival.

We are incredibly fortunate to be welcoming back our Armed Forces, who once again bring with them a host of military aircraft and assets.

There are a number of firsts this year, the Red Arrows displaying on all four days, the once in a lifetime flypast of the Canadian Lancaster with the Battle of Britain Memorial Flight, the Canberra and Blades performing during the extended dusk display. Not forgetting Festival favourites including the Sea Vixen, Miss Demeanour, a host of helicopters, beach assaults and huge naval presence including international participation with the French Navy's ship Sagittaire.

On behalf of the Festival organisers, a big thank you to everyone involved in helping to stage the event and putting in so much time and effort. Special thanks to the Patrons 100 Club Ambassador David Bailey of the Hotel Miramar, our Festival Maker volunteers and all those from the industry for their hard work, with Bournemouth Tourism, in developing the Air Festival into the hugely successful, event it is today. Finally, thank you all for your support, for the event and its nominated charities. We hope you enjoy 4-days of land, sea and air entertainment in the UK's premier resort.

GW00401470

AIR FESTIVAL TIMETABLE

FREE
UPDATED ONLINE
AIR DISPLAY TIMETABLE
WITH THIS BROCHURE

YOUR UNIQUE ACCESS CODE IS ENCLOSED

Bournemouth
BOROUGH COUNCIL

OFFICIAL EVENT

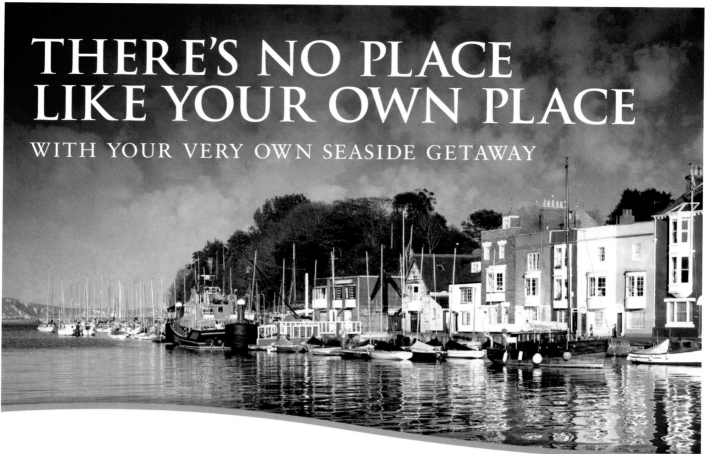

THERE'S NO PLACE LIKE YOUR OWN PLACE

WITH YOUR VERY OWN SEASIDE GETAWAY

Enjoy the Air Festival every year – and seaside holidays any time you like – in your very own luxury caravan at one of our two fabulous holiday parks.

Relax by the sea in beautiful Dorset, and enjoy the amazing advantages of owning your own holiday retreat.

Including:

- Choice of two fantastic locations
- Exclusive use of on-park facilities
- A wide range of financial options
- Subletting service – earn up to £10,000

Owner benefits include:

- FREE nightly entertainment
- FREE WiFi internet access
- FREE use of our sauna, gym and swimming pools
- 24-hour security

For more information or a brochure:

Call 01305 836836

or visit watersidegroupsales.co.uk

WATERSIDE HOLIDAY PARK & SPA   CHESILVISTA HOLIDAY PARK

Waterside Holiday Park and Spa, Bowleaze Cove, Weymouth, Dorset DT3 6PP • Chesil Vista Holiday Park, Portland Road, Weymouth, Dorset DT4 9AG

BEAUTIFUL BOURNEMOUTH

There is certainly no shortage of things to do with attractions, activities and year-round events to keep the whole family amused whatever the taste, age or budget, here are some dates for your diary.

ARTS BY THE SEA FESTIVAL
26th September - 12th October 2014

With an exciting 'on the edge' theme the 2-week Arts by the Sea Festival is not to be missed! Perfect for art enthusiasts, art lovers, creative individuals, families or those who are simply curious the Festival offers a great mix of award-winning performance, film, music and visual arts displayed across two jam-packed weeks. Official opening weekend (26th – 28th September) will feature Carabosse Fire Gardens, Fuel presenting The Roof and a vintage market. **artsbournemouth.org.uk**

BOURNEMOUTH MARATHON FESTIVAL
4th & 5th October 2014

Back for a second year running, the town is set to host the unique festival of running. Showcasing the best of Bournemouth athletes and fun runners, there will be a variety of different races for all abilities and for all of the family. **run-bmf.com**

CHRISTMAS LIGHT SWITCH ON AND CHRISTMAS FESTIVAL
November 23rd - early January 2015

Bournemouth's enchanting Christmas spirit officially comes alive on the 23rd November with the lights switch on.

Then, until early January, the town becomes a magical winter wonder land transformed into a twinkling bustling Christmas fantasy with merry live music, a fabulous festive bar and beautiful chalet market stalls. From the 29th November the Bournemouth Gardens of Light Festival offers a unique free five-week Christmas event featuring innovative and interactive lighting installations in Bournemouth's beautiful and historic gardens.

For more information check out **bournemouth.co.uk** email info@bournemouth.gov.uk or call **0845 051 1700**

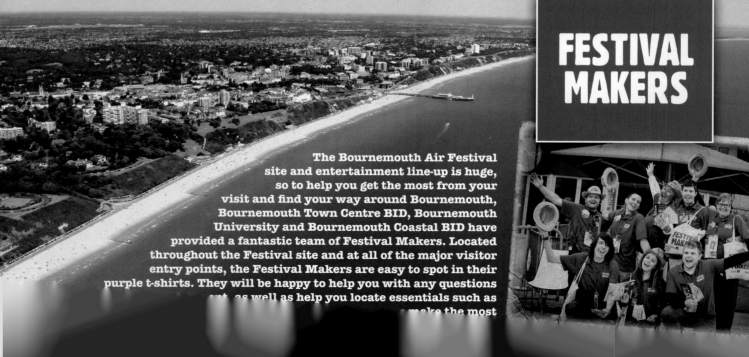

FESTIVAL MAKERS

The Bournemouth Air Festival site and entertainment line-up is huge, so to help you get the most from your visit and find your way around Bournemouth, Bournemouth Town Centre BID, Bournemouth University and Bournemouth Coastal BID have provided a fantastic team of Festival Makers. Located throughout the Festival site and at all of the major visitor entry points, the Festival Makers are easy to spot in their purple t-shirts. They will be happy to help you with any questions ... as well as help you locate essentials such as ... make the most

CHARITIES & PATRONS

Patrons evening at The Chine Hotel

Thank you for purchasing your official Bournemouth Air Festival brochure and supporting our charities with the 2014 wristband!

This year's nominated charities are The Not Forgotten Association, The British Lung Foundation, The Jon Egging Trust and The Royal Navy & Royal Marines Charity. £1 from every brochure sale and money raised by the 2014 wristband will be distributed between the four charities.

It's a big 'thank you' again to local businessman and Hot Rocks Managing Director John Green who has funded this year's wristband. Since 2011 we have raised nearly £60,000 for our charities, the challenge for 2014 is to raise £20,000 which will help us reach our target of £100,000 by the end of next year.

Not Forgotten Association

Founded shortly after WWI, The Not Forgotten Association works to support those whose lives have been affected by conflict or by subsequent injury. "We are delighted to be recognised and nominated as a 2014 Air Festival charity".

British Lung Foundation

The British Lung Foundation work hard to support anyone affected by lung disease so that no one has to face it alone. "We are delighted to have been selected as one of the beneficiaries of this year's Air Festival and we are incredibly grateful that the organisers are helping us achieve our mission."

The Jon Egging Trust

The Jon Egging Trust works to create partnerships and develop opportunities for young people who are under-achieving in the formal education system or those who are from disadvantaged backgrounds. "Being a beneficiary for the 3rd consecutive year, we are constantly overwhelmed by the level of support and money raised by the Air Festival."

Royal Navy & Royal Marines Charity

The Royal Navy and Royal Marines Charity is the principal, and chosen, charity of the Royal Navy. Last year it gave £7.3 million to people most in need: serving personnel, veterans and families.

FREE
UPDATED ONLINE AIR DISPLAY TIMETABLE
WITH THIS BROCHURE
....
YOUR UNIQUE ACCESS CODE IS ENCLOSED

The Not Forgotten Association
nfassociation.org
Registered Charity Number 1150541

In support of
British Lung Foundation
blf.org.uk
Registered Charity Number 326730

KEEP UPDATED...
Get all the latest Air Festival updates by following us on Twitter (#bmthairfest) and Facebook (facebook.com/bournemouthairfestival) or on Air Festival Radio (87.7FM) and Air Festival TV, both broadcasting throughout the event.

The Jon Egging Trust
joneggingtrust.com
Registered Charity Number 1148180

ROYAL NAVY & ROYAL MARINES CHARITY
Royal Navy & Royal Marines Charity
rnrmc.org.uk
Registered Charity Number 1117794

TURN TO PAGE 48 FOR FURTHER DETAILS OF:

NIGHT AIR AT THE PIERS 2014

RAF HC2 **CHINOOK** 🌐 raf.mod.uk/chinookdisplayteam

The unmistakeable 'wocka wocka' of the Chinook is one of the most distinctive sounds in the sky and it makes a welcome return to Bournemouth again this year.

The Chinook Display Team is made up of personnel from both Nos 18(B) and 27 Squadrons and is supported by a team of engineers from 18/27 Engineering Squadron, all based at RAF Odiham in Hampshire.

After an award-winning 2012/13 season, the

Chinook Display Team return for 2014 with a new display, combining some of last year's award-winning sequence with new, exciting, high-energy manoeuvres.

The RAF operates the largest fleet of Chinook Support Helicopters after the US Army, with a total of 34 HC2s, 6 HC2As and most recently 14 new HC6s.

The Chinook Wing forms the heavy-lift element of the Joint Helicopter Command (JHC) and is based at RAF Odiham.

Odiham supports three operational squadrons, No 7 Squadron, No 18

Squadron and No 27 Squadron, and the Operational Conversion Flight where new pilots and rear crew learn to operate the Chinook. The HC2 and HC2A aircraft are used primarily for trooping and for carrying internal and/or underslung loads and can carry up to 55 troops or 10 tonnes of freight.

The cabin is large enough to accommodate two Land Rovers, while the three underslung load hooks allow a huge flexibility in the type and number of loads that can be carried externally.

The crew consists of two pilots and two Weapon systems operators (WSOp(airloadmaster)).

RN **MERLIN HM1** 🌐 royalnavy.mod.uk/the-equipment/aircraft/helicopters/merlin-mk1

The Merlin HM1 is the Royal Navy's most modern aircraft and its primary role is anti-submarine warfare. Fitted with state-of-the art sensors and communications equipment, its technological capability has been proven on operations across the world.

Its size, speed and technology make it a truly versatile aircraft and its sophisticated flight control computers allow the pilot to

hover day and night, in extreme weather, from the flight decks of both large and small ships.

The Merlin's impressive radar can be used to track hundreds of miles away. It can lift heavy loads, and the submarine tracking equipment in the rear can easily be replaced with seats for carrying troops, search and rescue operations and casualty evacuation.

The Navy is in the process of upgrading its fleet to Mk2 Merlins. The Merlin has been in service with the Royal Navy for more than a decade, but is in the middle of a £750m revamp which will see the fleet of helicopters, all based at Royal Naval Air Station Culdrose in Cornwall, ready to take the fight to submarines until the end of the 2020s.

BACK FOR 2014!

WEYMOUTH SEA★LIFE
ADVENTURE PARK AND TOWER

NEW Octonauts Mission Briefing!

Don't miss our new Seal Harbour!

50% OFF!

For directions and opening times go to

SEALIFEWEYMOUTH.COM

V22334

IT'S TIME TO OWN YOUR OWN HOLIDAY HOME

With your own stunning lodge at one of our superior holiday parks, you can enjoy the Air Festival every year and the beautiful beaches, coastline and countryside any time you like!

Imagine all the comforts of home, in a brand new home from home – with all these extra benefits too:

Including:

- Choice of three fantastic locations
- Exclusive use of on-park facilities
- A wide range of financial options
- Lodge Owners Privilege card

Owner benefits include:

- Country Club and heated outdoor pool
- Spa and Leisure Club membership
- 24-hour security
- Highest spec lodges in the UK

For more information:

Call 01305 836842

email ben@watersideholidays.co.uk
or visit watersidegroupsales.co.uk

YOUR HOLIDAY HOME FROM HOME

Waterside Holiday Park and Spa, Weymouth, Dorset DT3 6PP • Chesil Vista Holiday Park, Weymouth, Dorset DT4 9AG • Osmington Holiday Park, Weymouth, Dorset DT3 6HB

ENGLISH ELECTRIC PR9
CANBERRA

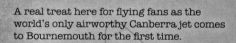

🌐 midair-squadron.com/canberra-xh134

🐦 twitter.com/midairsqn

f facebook.com/midairsquadron

A real treat here for flying fans as the world's only airworthy Canberra jet comes to Bournemouth for the first time.

It is operated by The Midair Squadron, which has a collection of three classic British aircraft, flying two Hawker Hunters alongside the Canberra.

This year is its first full display season since 2006, when this example, XH134, having astonishingly been in service since 1959.

She went virtually direct to Midair and had a few outings last year.

The Canberra, which was the RAF's first jet-powered bomber, entered service in 1951 – it was unarmed and relied on its speed to escape enemy fighters.

The English Electric Canberra was sold to air forces all over the world and a total 1,347 were built.

During its first 10 years of service with the RAF, the Canberra broke 19 flight records and three altitude records including winning the London to New Zealand Air Race in 1953 with a world speed record and the first jet flight over the North Pole in 1954.

The Canberra is believed to be the world's longest-serving bomber and most recently provided support during conflicts in the Balkans and Middle East.

And, because of its ability to fly at nearly 60,000 ft, it was also used for clandestine photo reconnaissance work during the Cold War. Incredibly, the aircraft only retired from active duty in 2006.

Fully restored with complete airworthiness certification, experienced engineering and maintenance support – and highly qualified senior RAF pilots – Canberra XH134 is the only air-worthy Canberra of its type in the world.

THE TEAM...

Flight Lieutenant Mike Leckey is chief pilot. In 1988 Mike joined the Royal Air Force and on completion of flying training in 1991, he was posted to fly the Canberra T17 on 360 Sqn. He remained here until 1994 when the Squadron was disbanded.

After completing the Qualified Flying Instructors course at Scampton and Cranwell, Mike was posted to Northumbrian Universities Air Squadron at Leeming. Here he gained his A2 instructors category and in 1997 was posted to 39 Sqn to be the Sqn QFI in

the Canberra PR9. Survey detachments to Zimbabwe and Norway soon followed along with operations in the Balkans and Iraq.

Whilst on 39 Sqn, Mike joined the Battle of Britain Memorial Flight and spent nine years displaying the Lancaster and Dakota.

TECHNICAL SPECIFICATION

ROLE: Bomber and clandestine reconnaissance
MANUFACTURER: English Electric
LENGTH: 20.4m (66ft, 8ins)
WINGSPAN: 20.7m (67ft, 10ins)
ENGINE: 2 x RR Avon Mk20601
MAX. SPEED: 518mph (450 knots)
MAX. FLIGHT HEIGHT: Over 18,288m (60,000ft)
ON BOARD CREW: One
RANGE: 2900nm
WEIGHT (MTOW): 23,133kg (51,000lbs)

Mike flew the last ever operational RAF Canberra sortie over Afghanistan. Mike is currently a Leadership Instructor at the RAF College, Cranwell.

Squadron Leader (Retd) Dave Piper is operations director and pilot.

Dave's long association with the Canberra began in 1979 on 360 Squadron at RAF Wyton, following pilot training on the Jet Provost, Hawk and Jetstream.

Promoted to Squadron Leader in 1992, he became the Officer Commanding the Multi-Engine Pilot Training Squadron, flying the Jetstream, initially from RAF Finningley and then

RAF Cranwell. In 2004, he returned to flying the ultimate Canberra variant, the PR9, operated by 39 Squadron at RAF Marham. During this time he became Flight Commander Operations and saw service across Europe, the Middle East and Afghanistan.

Dave flew over Buckingham Palace, in formation with the Red Arrows, as part of HRH Her Majesty the Queen's 80th birthday celebrations.

Retiring from the regular air force in 2011, Dave has since worked as a reservist flying instructor for the RAF. He now teaches Elementary Flying Training to the RAF's newest students.

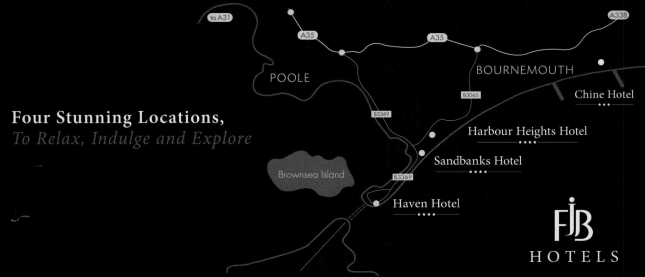

to A31

A35

A35

A338

POOLE

BOURNEMOUTH

B3065

Chine Hotel
★★★

Four Stunning Locations,
To Relax, Indulge and Explore

B3369

Harbour Heights Hotel
★★★★

Sandbanks Hotel
★★★★

Brownsea Island

B3369

Haven Hotel
★★★★

FJB
H O T E L S

Sponsors of the Air Festival 2014

Mouchel is once again sponsoring the Bournemouth Air Festival, an event which brings the community together, boosts the local area's economy, and is a lot of fun too!

Mouchel is focused on work that benefits the community. In fact, we have been working in partnership with Bournemouth Council since 2010 to help boost Bournemouth in a whole host of ways:

♦ We've created more than 100 local jobs, and have plans for creating many more over the coming years

♦ We're helping make your environment one that is eco-friendly, including installing solar panels on public buildings such as the pier entrance

♦ We're improving your local attractions, such as providing the IT for the new Hengistbury Head visitor centre

♦ We're re-designing and improving local schools' buildings, to ensure your children are getting the best learning environments possible

♦ We're working to improve your Council's services to make them more effective and customer-friendly

Mouchel will continue to work to bring a range of benefits to Bournemouth, but in the meantime we hope you all enjoy the Air Festival!

building great relationships

www.mouchel.com

THE ROYAL AIR FORCE
RED ARROWS
AEROBATIC DISPLAY TEAM

raf.mod.uk/reds

twitter.com/rafredarrows

facebook.com/royalairforceredarrows

IT'S a special year for Bournemouth Air Festival favourites the Red Arrows as the team celebrates 50 years of wowing crowds around the world.

This year the team's 'boss' – Red 1 – is once again Sqn Ldr Jim Turner, who is in his second spell with the team.

Its pilots are fast jet pilots from front line RAF squadrons and will return to their duties once their three year stint with the team is over.

Just to apply, a candidate has to meet basic requirements; a minimum of 1,500 flying hours, the completion of a front line tour and be assessed as 'above average'. During the display season, the Red Arrows will appear at up to 100 displays.

They promote the professional excellence of the Royal Air Force,

assist in recruiting into the Royal Air Force, contribute to Defence Diplomacy when displaying overseas and support wider British interests through the promotion of British industry by demonstrating the capabilities of its equipment and expertise.

The Red Arrows continue to enthral, captivate and inspire millions of people both in the UK and around the world with a series of displays and fly-pasts at a wide variety of events.

Officer Commanding Red Arrows Squadron is Wing Commander Neil Fraser. As Officer Commanding RAF Red Arrows, Neil has the responsibility for all Red Arrows flying, engineering, administrative and safety matters.

He ensures that the procedures followed by the team allow for safe and efficient flying.

TECHNICAL SPECIFICATION

ROLE: Advanced trainer aircraft
MANUFACTURER: BAE Systems
LENGTH: 12.43 m (40 ft 9 in)
WINGSPAN: 9.94 m (32 ft 7 in)
ENGINE: 1× Rolls-Royce Adour Mk. 951 turbofan with FADEC, 29 kN (6,500 lbf) 29 kN
MAX. SPEED: Mach 0.84 (638 mph; 554 knots)
MAX. FLIGHT HEIGHT: 13,565 m (44,500 ft)
ON BOARD CREW: Two
RANGE: 1,565 miles
WEIGHT (MTOW): 9,100 kg (20,000 lb)

mouchel

Supporting
Royal Air Force
Red Arrows
display appearance
Thursday & Saturday

MORGAN SINDALL

Supporting
Royal Air Force
Red Arrows
display appearance
Friday & Sunday

Buy with just £6,498 deposit with Help to Buy

- Two superb Show Apartments now available to view

- In a prime location approximately 400 yards from the beautiful, sandy beach

- Help to Buy* available – buy with just a 5% deposit

BOURNEMOUTH
Owls Road, Boscombe Spa Village
BH5 1FE

Solo & 1 bedroom apartments
from £129,950

Help to Buy

Marketing Suite and Show Apartments
open Thursday to Monday
10am – 5pm (Fridays 4pm)

0844 644 9498
lindenhomes.co.uk/breeze

QR scan me now

Linden HOMES

Taking mixology to new heights...

£3.75
COCKTAILS
5-7PM EVERY DAY

2mins walk from Bournemouth beach - opposite the BIC

1812, Exeter Road, Bournemouth, BH2 5AG   Tel: 01202 20 30 50
www.1812Bournemouth.com

eighteen twelve
1812
lounge bar & restaurant

MEET THE **TEAM**

ROYAL AIR FORCE RED ARROWS AEROBATIC 2014 DISPLAY TEAM

Red 1: Sqn Ldr Jim Turner

After serving throughout Europe, the Middle East, Canada, North America and Iraq, Jim became the RAF's Jaguar display pilot before joining the Red Arrows in 2005. He went on to fly as Synchro 2 in 2006 and as Synchro Leader in 2007. Later, he spent time in the Middle East teaching the Royal Saudi Air Force Aerobatic Team.

Red 2: Flt Lt Stewart Campbell

Having joined the RAF in 2003, Stew has been an instructor and was later the RAF Tucano display pilot. He later flew the Tornado with 617 Squadron (The Dambusters) and has flown tours in Afghanistan.

Red 3: Flt Lt Joe Hourston

After training, Joe was posted to the Tornado GR4 and 617 Squadron (The Dambusters). He served in Afghanistan and on exercise in North America. Recently, Joe has been back at RAF Valley instructing on the RAF's new jet trainer, the Hawk T2.

Red 4: Flt Lt Oliver Parr

Olly joined the RAF in 1999 and later flew the Tornado GR4, including two tours to Iraq. In 2009 he was posted back to 31 Sqn for a second time and completed a four-month tour of Afghanistan. This is Olly's second year in the Red Arrows; last year he was Red 2.

Red 5: Flt Lt Steve Morris

Steve joined the Royal Air Force in 2002 and went on to fly the Tornado GR4. Steve was involved in operations over Libya with IX(B) Squadron and took part in exercises in both the UK and North America. This is his second year on the team.

Red 6: Flt Lt James McMillan

James has served in Afghanistan and also participated in numerous exercises, both in the UK and overseas. In 2010 he was posted to the Harrier Operational Conversion Unit. This is James' third year on the team.

Red 7: Flt Lt Mark Lawson

Mark has flown the Tornado GR4 and enjoyed numerous detachments around the world. Mark has deployed in operations in Iraq, Afghanistan and over Libya. This is Mark's second year on the team; in 2013 he was Red 3.

Red 8: Flt Lt Martin Pert

In 2006, aged 25, Martin was the RAF Hawk solo display pilot. He later served on operations over Afghanistan and has also completed many large-scale exercises globally. This is Martin's third year on the team.

Red 9: Flt Lt Mike Child

Mike was the Hawk display pilot in 2007. Having completed his Tactical Weapons Training, Mike was posted to the Typhoon. He was declared combat-ready in December 2009 and went on to serve on Quick Reaction Alert in the UK and the Falklands. Mike is in his third year with the team.

Red 10: Sqn Ldr Mike Ling
Team Supervisor

Mike joined the Red Arrows in 2008 before being selected for the Synchro Pair for 2009 and 2010. Mike is in his third year as Red 10 and it's his sixth season with the team.

THE CIRCUS

Nine aircraft engineering technicians are chosen to form a team known as The Circus. Engineers are each allocated to a pilot for the duration of the season. They fly in the passenger seat of the Hawk and service the aircraft before and after every display. Once the display season is over, they return to their normal squadron duties.

Make moving a reality
We will help your dreams take off!

Whether you're looking or selling, whether your ideal home is a new apartment, a period property or anything in between, with the help of Hearnes Estate Agents you can look forward to finding what you want, finding a serious buyer and enjoying a smooth, successful transaction from beginning to end.

Bournemouth | 122 Old Christchurch Rd, Bournemouth BH1 1LU | 01202 317317 | bournemouth@hearnes.com
Ferndown | 390 Ringwood Rd, Ferndown BH22 9AU | 01202 890890 | ferndown@hearnes.com
Ringwood | 52-54 High St, Ringwood BH24 1AG | 01425 489955 | ringwood@hearnes.com
Wimborne | 6 Cook Row, Wimborne BH21 1LB | 01202 842922 | wimborne@hearnes.com

www.hearnes.com

de HAVILLAND
SEA VIXEN
DN110 FAW

Making a welcome return to the Bournemouth Air Festival fold in 2014 s a jet with plenty of local connections.

The de Havilland DN110 Sea Vixen FAW lives at Bournemouth Airport, where she is lovingly maintained by the same team that restored her to her current glory.

And now she is a firm favourite thanks to her slick, high-speed manoeuvres and the ear-splitting howl of her twin Rolls Royce Avon engines.

The Sea Vixen arrived at local company DS Aviation Ltd, then called de Havilland Aviation, 13 years ago. After five painstaking years of hard work she became, and remains, the only airworthy example of her kind in the world.

The versatile Vixen, originally built as a supersonic fighter, could carry all airborne weapons up to nuclear bombs as well as fulfilling the role of in-flight tanker.

Nowadays the Sea Vixen holds the honour of being the fastest privately owned aircraft in Europe, capable of flying at supersonic speeds.

MISS DEMEANOUR

heritageaviation.com

Appearance supported by

Marriott
BOURNEMOUTH HIGHCLIFF

By now the eye-catching Miss Demeanour needs little introduction to the Bournemouth faithful. A firm favourite with the crowds, you'll hear the Hunter jet coming with its distinctive screaming howl as it flashes into view.

Miss Demeanour was restored at Bournemouth Airport 16 years ago and looks and sounds like a rocket.

Owned and piloted by Jonathon Whaley, she made her debut in 2010

Jonathon is now semi-retired and has Miss Demeanour up for sale – he has lined up two pilots to fly her at the festival.

Originally built for the RAF in 1956, Miss Demeanour was delivered to Kemble in Gloucestershire before entering service with No 3 (Fighter) Squadron in Germany.

At the end of her RAF career she was transferred to the Fleet Air Arm at Arbroath as a ground instructional airframe before being put up for disposal. But that wasn't the end, she had a spell with the Swiss Air Force and in private ownership before Jonathon's company, Heritage Aviation Developments Ltd, acquired her in 1997, to restore her at Bournemouth Airport, the project being completed in mid-1998.

MORGAN SINDALL
INVESTMENTS

COLLABORATION AT THE HEART OF CONSTRUCTION

Morgan Sindall Investments Ltd are working alongside their sister companies Morgan Sindall plc and Lovell to provide a collaborative approach to construction. The MS Group of companies have extensive experience in construction and regeneration with a proven track record for delivery. As a partner of Bournemouth Development Company, MSIL are committed to ensure Bournemouth remains a vibrant and sustainable community.

MORGAN SINDALL GROUP
MORGAN SINDALL LOVELL

Madeira Road Car Park
382 space multi storey car park completed in February 2014

Madeira Road Student Accommodation
378-room student accommodation for the Arts University, Bournemouth Due for completion August 2014, for the new academic year

The Citrus Building
Contemporary studio, 1, 2 & 3 bedroom apartments in the heart of Bournemouth

msinvestments.co.uk

THE CITRUS BUILDING
BOURNEMOUTH

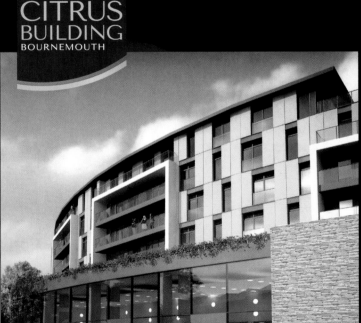

BOURNEMOUTH | MADEIRA ROAD BH1 1AR

TOWN CENTRE LIVING IN STYLE – IF YOU'RE QUICK!

All you need to buy a stunning new 2 bedroom apartment, with en suite and family bathroom, is a deposit of just £10,250 with Help to Buy.

The studios and apartments, some with a sunny balcony, feature state-of-the-art design and specification, including fabulous fitted kitchens and contemporary bathrooms – as you'd expect in this prime location.

FINAL STUDIO APARTMENT REMAINING

**Help to Buy available –
5% deposit, 75% mortgage, 100% your home***

STUDIO, 1, 2 & 3 BEDROOM APARTMENTS FROM £130,000

Show Home open Thursday to Monday 10am – 5pm

Call Stubbings Property Marketing **01628 482276**

 thecitrusbuilding.co.uk 01628 482276 citrusbuilding @citrusbuilding

A Proud Partnership between
Bournemouth Borough Council & Morgan Sindall Investments

BournemouthDevelopmentCompany

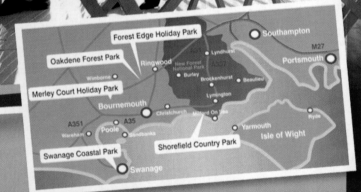

XH558 AVRO VULCAN

vulcantothesky.org

twitter.com/xh558

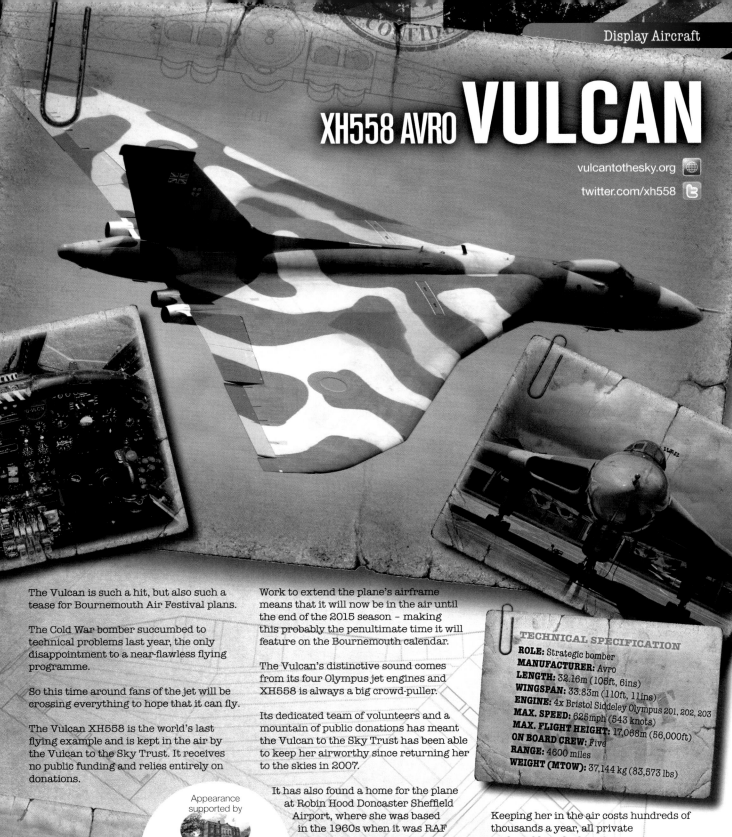

The Vulcan is such a hit, but also such a tease for Bournemouth Air Festival plans.

The Cold War bomber succumbed to technical problems last year, the only disappointment to a near-flawless flying programme.

So this time around fans of the jet will be crossing everything to hope that it can fly.

The Vulcan XH558 is the world's last flying example and is kept in the air by the Vulcan to the Sky Trust. It receives no public funding and relies entirely on donations.

Appearance
supported by

Merley House
Wedding and Function Venue
In association with Stephen Young
Lord of Westbury and Vulcan To The
Sky Team Bournemouth

Work to extend the plane's airframe means that it will now be in the air until the end of the 2015 season – making this probably the penultimate time it will feature on the Bournemouth calendar.

The Vulcan's distinctive sound comes from its four Olympus jet engines and XH558 is always a big crowd-puller.

Its dedicated team of volunteers and a mountain of public donations has meant the Vulcan to the Sky Trust has been able to keep her airworthy since returning her to the skies in 2007.

It has also found a home for the plane at Robin Hood Doncaster Sheffield Airport, where she was based in the 1960s when it was RAF Finningley.

It is now hoped that there is a real opportunity to create a permanent home for the aircraft and that something special could be created there to fulfil the objective of the Trust to educate and inspire young people.

The effort to get her back in the air started in 1997; it took 10 years and £7 million before she once more took to the skies in 2007.

TECHNICAL SPECIFICATION

ROLE: Strategic bomber
MANUFACTURER: Avro
LENGTH: 32.16m (105ft, 6ins)
WINGSPAN: 33.83m (110ft, 11ins)
ENGINE: 4x Bristol Siddeley Olympus 201, 202, 203
MAX. SPEED: 625mph (543 knots)
MAX. FLIGHT HEIGHT: 17,068m (56,000ft)
ON BOARD CREW: Five
RANGE: 4600 miles
WEIGHT (MTOW): 37,144 kg (83,573 lbs)

Keeping her in the air costs hundreds of thousands a year, all private cash and largely donations.

The Avro Vulcan is a delta wing subsonic jet bomber that was operated by the Royal Air Force from 1953 until 1984. It was designed in the late 1940s by the team that created the WW2 Lancaster bomber.

XH558 is the only flying Vulcan in the world and is also the oldest complete Vulcan anywhere, representing the 300-plus bombers which made up the UK's contribution to the NATO strategy of deterrence.

ROYAL Battle of Britain
AIR FORCE Memorial Flight

BBMF
SPITFIRE

This hero of WWII needs little introduction. It was produced in greater numbers than any other British combat aircraft.

In a 12-year period there were no less than 22 variants – not including the Royal Navy version – and 20,400 planes rolled off the line.

The prototype was developed from the Supermarine seaplane designed by RJ Mitchell to win the Schneider trophy and the maiden flight took place on March 5th, 1936.

It was during the dogfights over southern England during the Battle of Britain that the Spitfire earned its place in history, staving off the Luftwaffe.

They remained in RAF front-line service until 1954. The Battle of Britain Memorial Flight operates five survivors. Two of them were produced near the end of the war for high level reconnaissance.

One could hit speeds of 370mph and reach an altitude of 40,000 feet; higher than the cruising altitude of a modern commercial jet. Another, P7350, is the oldest flying Spitfire in the world and survived a crash landing during the Battle of Britain.

Appearance supported by
PREMIUM
SPITFIRE
KENTISH ALE

🌐 raf.mod.uk/bbmf/theaircraft/spitfirehistory.cfm

🌐 raf.mod.uk/bbmf/theaircraft/hurricane.cfm

BBMF
HURRICANE

Perhaps unfairly overshadowed in history by the Spitfire, the Hurricane is one of the classic fighters of all time.

Designed and built for war, it was at the forefront of Britain's defence in 1939/1940 and it played a major part in achieving victory in 1945.

The prototype made its maiden flight on 6th November 1935 and deliveries to the RAF commenced just before Christmas 1937 (to 111 Squadron at Northolt).

During the Battle of Britain, RAF Fighter Command fielded more Hurricanes than Spitfires, and Hurricanes achieved a similarly greater proportion of combat kills during the battle.

A remarkable total of 14,533 Hurricanes were built and the aircraft served operationally on every day throughout hostilities, in every operational theatre and in many roles.

At the end of WWII in 1945, Hurricanes were still in the front-line helping to ensure final victory in the Far East.

Appearance supported by
PREMIUM
SPITFIRE
KENTISH ALE

BRITAIN SHALL NEVER BE SLAVES

'Cos that is actually illegal.

The **BOTTLE** of **BRITAIN**   ISN'T IT. ISN'T IT THOUGH.

f /spitfireale

BBMF **LANCASTER**

raf.mod.uk/bbmf/theaircraft/lancaster.cfm

The Battle of Britain Memorial Flight will bring Lancaster bomber PA474 back to its former home county of Dorset.

She was built in Chester in 1945 and was earmarked for use in the Far East.

But after Japan surrendered, she had spells as a reconnaissance plane in Africa, and was then loaned to Flight Refuelling Ltd at Tarrant Rushton, Blandford.

She had several more RAF jobs and joined the Battle of Britain Memorial Flight in November 1973. Today she is one of only two Lancasters still in airworthy condition in the World.

The first production model Lancaster flew in 1941 and it was the mainstay of the British night-time bombing offensive over Germany.

Almost half of all Lancasters delivered during the war (3,345 out of 7,373) were lost on operations with the loss of more than over 21,000 crew members.

This year there will be a special treat as, along with the Canadian Lancaster that is displaying, crowds will be able to see the only two airworthy Lancasters in the sky.

TECHNICAL SPECIFICATION

ROLE: Heavy Bomber
MANUFACTURER: Avro
LENGTH: 21.18 meters (69 feet 5 inches)
WINGSPAN: 31.09 meters (102 feet)
ENGINE: 4 x Rolls Royce Merlin XX V12
Max. Speed: 280 mph (243 knots)
Max. Flight height: 7,162m (23,600 ft)
ON BOARD CREW: 7 pilot, flight engineer, navigator, bomb aimer/nose gunner, wireless operator, mid-upper and rear gunners
Range: 2,530 miles
WEIGHT (MTOW): 32,727kg (72,000lb)

Appearance supported by **PREMIUM SPITFIRE** KENTISH ALE

TECHNICAL SPECIFICATION

Role: Military transport
Manufacturer: Douglas Aircraft Company
Length: 19.7m (64ft, 8ins)
Wingspan: 29m (95ft, 2ins)
Engine: 2 × Pratt & Whitney R-1830-90C Twin Wasp 14-cylinder radial engines, 1,200 hp (895 kW) each
Max. Speed: 230mph (200 knots)
Max. Flight height: 7,100m (23,200ft)
On board crew: Two
Range: 1,600 miles
Weight (MTOW): 14,061kg (31,000lbs)

BBMF DAKOTA

This year the Dakota is making an appearance alongside the regular Lancaster, Spitfire and Hurricane.

The Douglas C-47 Dakota is without doubt one of the most successful aircraft designs in history.

It became one of the world's most famous military transport aircraft and saw widespread use by the Allies during WWII- and subsequently by Air Forces and civilian operators worldwide.

The C-47 is a military version of the DC-3 airliner, which first flew in 1935 and was used extensively thereafter by America's airlines.

Recognizing the DC-3's great potential as a military transport, the United States Army Air Command specified a number of changes needed to make the aircraft suitable for military use, including more powerful engines, the replacement of airline seating with utility seats along the

raf.mod.uk/bbmf/theaircraft/dakota.cfm

walls, a stronger load-bearing floor and the addition of large loading doors.

Deliveries of the military version of the DC-3, which was designated C-47 'Skytrain' in the United States, commenced in October 1941. When production finally ended, a remarkable 10,692 DC-3/C-47 aircraft had been built.

Under the lend lease programme large scale deliveries of C-47s were made to the UK, with nearly 2,000 Dakotas, as the aircraft became known in RAF service, being delivered, the first entering service with the RAF in India in 1942.

The delivery of large numbers of Dakota IIIs revitalised the RAF's transport capacity, which until then had been based around a number of obsolete bombers and general purpose aircraft, which were poorly adapted for the role.

The Dakota III eventually equipped twenty two RAF squadrons and three RCAF squadrons under RAF operational control.

Dakotas served in every theatre of the war, most notably in Burma and also during the D-Day landings and the airborne assault on Arnhem in 1944. As a tactical transport aircraft, the Dakota was used to carry troops and freight, for the air-dropping of supplies and paratroops, for towing gliders and for casualty evacuation.

The Dakota 's amazing ruggedness became legendary and under the demands of war its capabilities were increased to permit it to carry a payload more than double the original specification or 28 fully-equipped soldiers or paratroops. In practice, the aircraft's specified limits were often exceeded.

CANADIAN **LANCASTER**

An historic event is set to take place at this year's air festival, with the arrival of the Canadian Lancaster.

It means that the world's only two airworthy examples of the bomber will fly together for the first, and probably last, time.

The second Lancaster is from Canada and flown by the Canadian Warplane Heritage Museum (CWHM).

It is spending a month-and-a-half in the UK and is taking part in several events with the BBMF.

The aircraft left Hamilton, Ontario, on August 4 and arrived in England on August 8, following a north Atlantic crossing that included stops at Goose Bay, Labrador, Canada, Narsarsuaq, Greenland, and Keflavik in Iceland.

Canadian Warplane Heritage Museum President and CEO, Squadron Leader (Ret.) David G. Rohrer C.D. who is a current Lancaster pilot, added: "This is a special salute to all the veterans of Bomber Command".

"On behalf of the team and all involved we are really looking forward to displaying for the Bournemouth Air Festival".

The Museum's Lancaster Mk. X was built at Victory Aircraft, Malton, in July 1945 and was later converted to a RCAF 10MR configuration.

In 1952 it suffered a serious accident and received a replacement wing centre section from a Lancaster that had flown in combat over Germany. It served as a maritime patrol aircraft, with No. 405 Squadron, Greenwood, NS and No. 107

Rescue Unit, Torbay, Newfoundland for many years and was retired from the RCAF in late 1963.

With help from the Sulley Foundation in 1977, it was acquired from the Royal Canadian Legion in Goderich, Ontario, where it had been on outside display.

Eleven years passed before it was completely restored and flew again on September 24, 1988.

The Lancaster is dedicated to the memory of P/O Andrew Mynarski and is referred to as the "Mynarski Memorial Lancaster".

It is painted in the colours of his aircraft KB726 – VR-A, which flew with RCAF No. 419 (Moose) Squadron.

Andrew Mynarski won the Victoria Cross, the Commonwealth's highest award for gallantry, on June 13, 1944, when his Lancaster was shot down in flames by a German night fighter.

As the bomber fell, he attempted to free the tail gunner trapped in the rear turret of the blazing and out of control aircraft. The tail gunner miraculously survived the crash and lived to tell the story, but sadly Andrew Mynarski died from his severe burns.

twitter.com/CWHM

warplane.com/lancaster-2014-uk-tour.aspx

facebook.com/CanadianWarplaneHeritageMuseum

A CAREER WITHOUT EQUAL

Bournemouth Crew Training Centre DROP IN 30/31 August

Life as an airline pilot is truly unique – challenge, variety and exhilaration all rolled into one.

CTC WINGS – THE route to the airline flight deck.

We are opening our Crew Training Centre – Bournemouth up for visitors on 30/31 August. Why not drop in on your way to the beach?

Tickets can be booked through our website. Our team will also be on stand on the esplanade throughout the air festival 28-31 August.

Discover more and be inspired: ctcaviation.com/wings

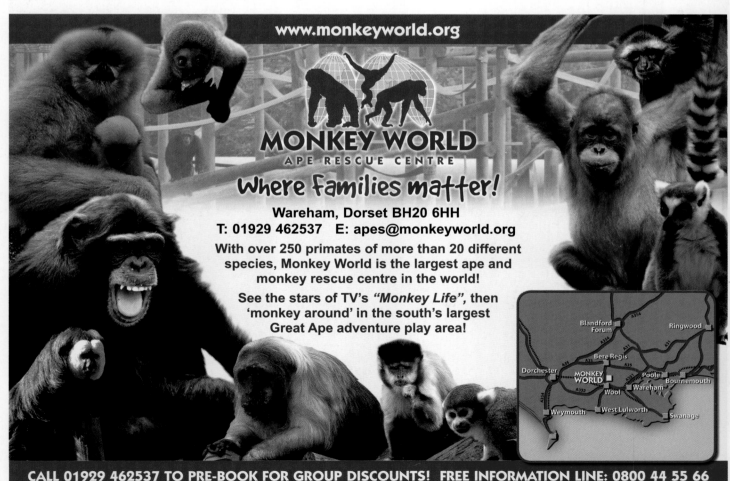

THE ROYAL AIR FORCE
TYPHOON

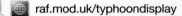

raf.mod.uk/typhoondisplay

twitter.com/RAFTyphoonTeam

facebook.com/raftyphoon

Appearance
supported by
CityFibre

Alongside the Red Arrows and the Vulcan, the Typhoon is one of the most highly-anticipated displays at the air festival and it makes a welcome return this year.

This year's team, from No 29 (Reserve) Squadron from RAF Coningsby, comprises a specialist from every aircraft trade along with support and management teams to assist both the pilot and the trades, all of whom work closely together to bring you the dazzling spectacle that is the Typhoon Display.

Every member of the team has been hand-picked from what is already an elite cadre of skilled personnel at RAF Coningsby.

They have proven themselves in their day jobs and are now privileged and proud to represent the very best in excellence and dedication that the Royal Air Force can offer.

In 2008 the Typhoon became the first and only current RAF fast jet to be declared Multi-Role capable.

Typhoon has increased significantly the RAF's war fighting capability and is an exceptionally flexible and capable aircraft.

Typhoon can carry out precision ground attack or air defence tasks and has the ability to support operations anywhere in the world.

Typhoon will provide the backbone of RAF fast jet operations for many years to come.

The Typhoon is a multi-role combat aircraft, capable of performing the full spectrum of air operations: from air policing, to peace support through to high intensity conflict.

As with other fast jets in the RAF, Typhoon can deliver weapons quickly and with a very high degree of accuracy; however, it is unique in being able to utilise its own inherent air-to-air capability to fight its way to the target without having to rely on additional, dedicated fighters for protection.

It is also capable of delivering a large number of weapons accurately as a close air support platform in aid of troops on the ground.

The Typhoon's airframe is both lightweight and durable due to modern manufacturing techniques and owing to the use of composite materials. Seventy percent of the airframe structure is made from Carbon Fibre Composite (CFC). A further 15 per cent utilises metal (titanium and aluminium alloys), the remaining percentage being taken up by 12 per cent Glass Reinforced Plastic (GRP) and lastly three per cent acrylics.

The Typhoon has a delta wing configuration, this combined with the unique foreplane stability system gives the aircraft agility (+9/-3g), high lift and STOL (Short Take Off & Landing) performance while still maintaining a low drag co-efficient.

The aircraft is equipped with the ECR90 radar and an advanced integrated defensive aids system. The pilot can carry out many aircraft functions by voice activation and 'Hands on Throttle and Stick' (HOTAS) commands whilst simultaneously manoeuvring the aircraft.

The Typhoon's 13 armament hard points (and gun) can be utilised to carry a multitude of weapons from the NATO inventory.

When fully loaded the aircraft can climb to 35,000 ft from releasing the brakes in 90 seconds and climb to a service ceiling beyond 55,000 ft due to the phenomenal performance of the EJ200 power plant.

TECHNICAL SPECIFICATION

Role: Multirole fighter
Manufacturer: Eurofighter
Length: 15.96 m (52.4 ft)
Wingspan: 10.95 m (35.9 ft)
Engine: 2 × Eurojet EJ200 afterburning turbofan
Max. Speed: Mach 2 (1,522mph; 1,322 knots)
Max. Flight height: 19,812m (65,000 ft)
On board crew: One operational, two training
Range: 1,800 miles
Weight (MTOW): 23,500 kg (51,800 lb)

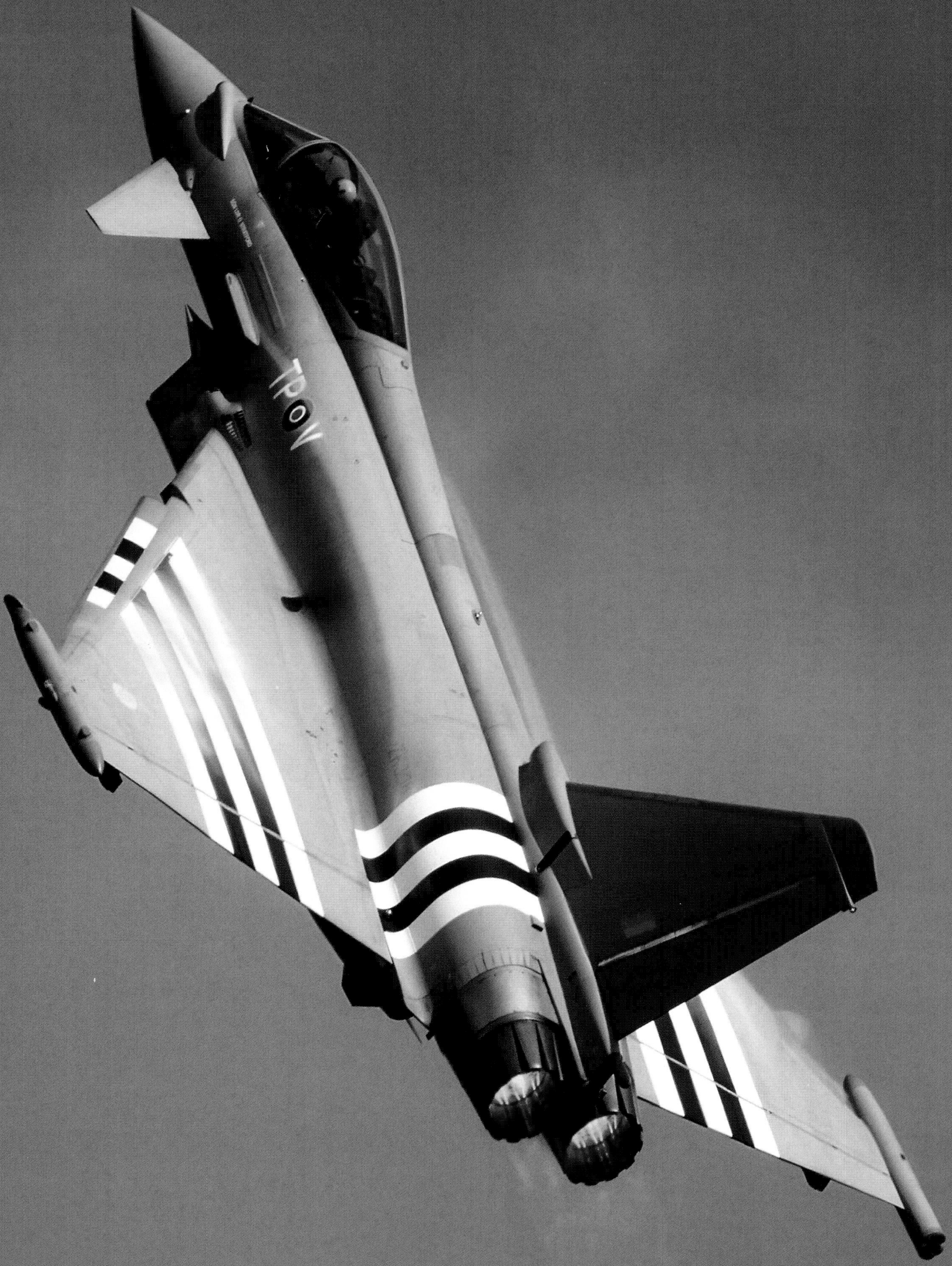

campbell
rowley

Proud sponsors of

**Bournemouth
Air Festival** 2014

Campbell Rowley Ltd
40 Holdenhurst Road
Bournemouth BH8 8AD

01202 551116
studio@campbellrowley.co.uk
@campbellrowley

campbellrowley.com

DESIGN
BRANDING
PHOTOGRAPHY
DIGITAL

DAILY EVENT TIMETABLE

THURSDAY 28th

BOURNEMOUTH AIR FESTIVAL

1.25pm – 2.30pm...

AEROBATICS
WING WALKER TOM LACKEY
95 year old record breaker!

FLYING DISPLAY
FLYING SCHOLARSHIPS FOR DISABLED PEOPLE

FLYING SCHOLARSHIPS
FSDP
for disabled people

FLYING DISPLAY
ROYAL NAVY BLACK CATS
HELICOPTER DISPLAY TEAM

PARACHUTE DISPLAY TEAM
ROYAL AIR FORCE FALCONS

FLYING DISPLAY
ROYAL AIR FORCE TUTOR T1

FLYING DISPLAY
ROYAL AIR FORCE CHINOOK

2.30pm – 4.00pm...

FLYING DISPLAY
RAF BATTLE OF BRITAIN MEMORIAL FLIGHT

FLYING DISPLAY
RAF BBMF DAKOTA C-47

FLYING DISPLAY
ROYAL NAVY MERLIN HM1

3.15pm
AEROBATIC
RAF AEROBATIC TEAM THE RED ARROWS

FLYING DISPLAY
ROYAL AIR FORCE TUCANO T1

FLYING DISPLAY
ROLLS ROYCE SPITFIRE

Bournemouth
BOROUGH COUNCIL
OFFICIAL EVENT

Disclaimer: Please note that flying times are correct at the time of going to print. All aircraft are subject to availability and weather conditions. No responsibility can be taken for any cancellations to the flying programme.

DAILY EVENT TIMETABLE

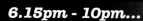

BOURNEMOUTH AIR FESTIVAL

THURSDAY 28th

7.15pm - 8.40pm...

NIGHT AIR AT THE PIERS

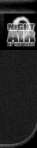

NIGHT AIR
AEROBATICS

ROLLS ROYCE SPITFIRE

NIGHT AIR
AEROBATICS

O'BRIEN'S FLYING CIRCUS

NIGHT AIR
AEROBATICS

SOLO TWISTER

NIGHT AIR
AEROBATICS

RED DEVILS
PARACHUTE DISPLAY TEAM

6.15pm - 10pm...

6.15pm - 6.25pm
EAST OVERCLIFF
ROYAL MARINES COMMANDO RECRUITING TEAM

6.30pm - 6.55pm
EAST OVERCLIFF
ROYAL MARINES THE BEAT RETREAT

6.30pm - 9.00pm
LOWER GARDENS
CIRCUS WORKSHOP, HULA HOOPING, FACE PAINTING AND PUNCH & JUDY

7.00pm - 9.00pm
LOWER GARDENS BANDSTAND
ARMY AIR CORPS BAND
6 PIECE ROCK POP COMBO

Corona Extra

8.30pm -10.00pm
BOURNEMOUTH PIER STAGE
SILVER BEATLES
TRIBUTE ACT

FREE
UPDATED ONLINE AIR DISPLAY TIMETABLE WITH THIS BROCHURE

YOUR UNIQUE ACCESS CODE IS ENCLOSED

AIR FESTIVAL TV SPONSORED BY

Mansell Homes

DAILY EVENT TIMETABLE

FRIDAY 29th

12.30pm - 12.35pm...

FLYING DISPLAY
FLYING SCHOLARSHIPS FOR DISABLED PEOPLE

1.20pm - 2.30pm...

FLYING DISPLAY
ARMY AIR CORPS LYNX

PARACHUTE DISPLAY TEAM
ROYAL AIR FORCE FALCONS

FLYING DISPLAY
ROYAL NAVY BLACK CATS
HELICOPTER DISPLAY TEAM

FLYING DISPLAY
ROYAL AIR FORCE TUTOR T1

FLYING DISPLAY
ROYAL AIR FORCE TUCANO T1

2.30pm - 4.05pm...

FLYING DISPLAY
RAF BATTLE OF BRITAIN MEMORIAL FLIGHT

FLYING DISPLAY
RAF BBMF DAKOTA C-47

3pm
AEROBATIC
RAF AEROBATIC TEAM THE RED ARROWS

FLYING DISPLAY
ROYAL AIR FORCE CHINOOK

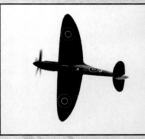

FLYING DISPLAY
ROLLS ROYCE SPITFIRE

FLYING DISPLAY
B-17 SALLY-B FLYING FORTRESS

FREE
UPDATED ONLINE AIR DISPLAY TIMETABLE WITH THIS BROCHURE
YOUR UNIQUE ACCESS CODE IS ENCLOSED

OFFICIAL EVENT

DAILY EVENT TIMETABLE

📻 Listen to Air Festival Radio: 87.7FM   🎤 Commentary by George Bacon and Andy Robbins

4.05pm - 4.40pm...

FLYING DISPLAY
HUNTER JET: MISS DEMEANOUR

FLYING DISPLAY
ROYAL NAVY MERLIN HM1

FLYING DISPLAY
ROYAL AIR FORCE TYPHOON FGR4

6.15pm - 10pm...

6.15pm - 6.25pm
EAST OVERCLIFF
ROYAL MARINES COMMANDO RECRUITING TEAM

6.30pm - 6.55pm
EAST OVERCLIFF
ROYAL MARINES THE BEAT RETREAT

6.30pm - 9.00pm
LOWER GARDENS
CIRCUS WORKSHOP, STILT WALKING, FACE PAINTING AND PUNCH & JUDY

7.15pm - 8.35pm...

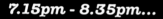

NIGHT AIR AEROBATICS
RR SPITFIRE & THE BLADES

NIGHT AIR AEROBATICS
O'BRIEN'S FLYING CIRCUS

NIGHT AIR AEROBATICS
SOLO TWISTER & RED DEVILS
PARACHUTE DISPLAY TEAM

7.00pm - 9.00pm
LOWER GARDENS BANDSTAND
ARMY AIR CORPS BAND
6 PIECE ROCK POP COMBO

7.00pm - 10.00pm
NIGHT AIR: BOSCOMBE STAGE
RIZZLE KICKS, LOVEABLE ROGUES, ALEXA GODDARD & RIXTON
TICKET ONLY EVENT

8.30pm - 10.00pm
NIGHT AIR: BOURNEMOUTH STAGE
BOOTLEG BLONDIE
TRIBUTE ACT

FRIDAY 29th

Don't forget...
FIREWORKS near Bournemouth Pier at 10pm

AIR FESTIVAL TV SPONSORED BY **MansellHomes**

Boscombe Pier: Corona Live Music Stage, presented by Wave 105 are ticketed only performance events. Tickets on sale Saturday 26th July 2014. Subject to availability. See bhlivetickets.co.uk

bournemouthair.co.uk powered by Campbell Rowley

41

Air Festival Site Map

Horseshoe Common

Lansdowne

NINTENDO 3DS & 2DS
made for play tour 2014

ROYAL AIR FORCE

NIGHT AIR AT THE PIERS 2014

Hot Rocks Restaurant & Bar

The Square
Obscura Café

Lower Gardens ZONE 4

Bournemouth Tourist Information
Bournemouth Balloon
Westover Road

Bath Hill

East Cliff

BIC Roundabout

The Pavilion Theatre
Pavilion Dance
Bath Hill Roundabout
Russell-Cotes Art Gallery & Museum

Pier Approach
Bournemouth Internat

BOURNEMOUTH EAST BEACH

ZONE 3

BOURNEMOUTH WEST BEACH

Stage

ZONE 5

The Pier

Bournemouth Pier

WESTBEACH

NIGHT AIR AT THE PIERS 2014
Corona Extra
Barny
Samsung Curved UHD TV
HARIBO

MUSIC STAGE

Pier to Pier - approx 25min walk

Falconry UK

Beat Retreat

Boscombe Pier

Boscombe Beach

ZONE 1

BOSCOMBE WEST BEACH

Stage

ONE 6

E 2

al

ine

MANOR ROAD

ST OVERCLIFF DRIVE

UNDERCLIFF DRIVE

UNDERCLIFF ROAD

DERBY ROAD

CHRISTCHURCH ROAD

CHRISTCHURCH ROAD

MANOR ROAD

ST. JOHN'S ROAD

OWLS ROAD

OWLS ROAD

SEA ROAD

ST. JOHN'S ROAD

HORACE ROAD

ARGYLL ROAD

BOSCOMBE SPA ROAD

WHARNCLIFFE ROAD

MICHELGROVE ROAD

BOSCOMBE SPA ROAD

7

'Set Yourself Free'
'THE FREE FROM TOUR' COMES TO MALVERN
Promoting a range of Great Tasting Healthy Alternative Foods

pure   fria   ocado.com   Vive soy   THE CHA CO

GLUTEN FREE - LACTOSE FREE - SUGAR FREE - WHEAT FREE
Try before you Buy   Come to Stand No 181 Avenue D

Koh Lounge

TANK HEROES

little tikes

Corona Extra
MUSIC STAGE WITH
wave 105.2 FM

BBC RADIO SOLENT
96J FM | 103.8 FM | DAB

wave 105.2 FM
the south's best variety of hits

ROYAL NAVY

ARMY

Map Key:

 Information

 First Aid

 Toilets

 Air Festival TV

 Road closure for spectators

 Cliff Lifts

 Park & Ride drop off and pick up point

 Hospitality

 Catering

 Funfair

 Disabled Parking

*Trading is between the Piers and is on the East Overcliff
**Map is a representation and not to scale
© Copyright Bournemouth Tourism

#bmthairfest   **f** facebook.com/bournemouthairfestival

SATURDAY 30th

12.30pm - 2.20pm...

SEAFRONT 11.25am - 11.40am
ROYAL MARINES COMMANDO RECRUITING TEAM

12.30pm - 12.35pm
FLYING SCHOLARSHIPS FOR DISABLED PEOPLE

BEACH
SEAFRONT IN FRONT OF RN & ARMY VILLAGE
ROYAL MARINES COMMANDO ASSAULT

FLYING DISPLAY
ROYAL AIR FORCE TYPHOON FGR4

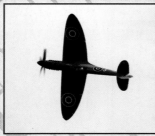

FLYING DISPLAY
ROLLS ROYCE SPITFIRE

FLYING DISPLAY
ROYAL NAVY BLACK CATS
HELICOPTER DISPLAY TEAM

FLYING DISPLAY
ROYAL AIR FORCE TUTOR T1

2.20pm - 3.35pm...

FLYING DISPLAY
ROYAL AIR FORCE TUCANO T1

FLYING DISPLAY
RAF BBMF MEMORIAL FLIGHT & CANADIAN LANCASTER

FLYING DISPLAY
RAF BBMF DAKOTA C-47

FLYING DISPLAY
ROYAL AIR FORCE CHINOOK

FLYING DISPLAY
ARMY AIR CORPS LYNX

PARACHUTE DISPLAY TEAM
THE TIGERS

FREE
UPDATED ONLINE AIR DISPLAY TIMETABLE
WITH THIS BROCHURE

YOUR UNIQUE ACCESS CODE IS ENCLOSED

OFFICIAL EVENT

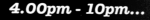
BOURNEMOUTH AIR FESTIVAL

SATURDAY 30th

3.35pm - 5.00pm...

FLYING DISPLAY
B-17 SALLY-B FLYING FORTRESS

FLYING DISPLAY
HUNTER JET: MISS DEMEANOUR

FLYING DISPLAY
ROYAL NAVY MERLIN HM1

FLYING DISPLAY
THE VULCAN

4.35pm
AEROBATIC
RAF AEROBATIC TEAM THE RED ARROWS

4.00pm - 10pm...

4.00pm - 5.00pm
LOWER GARDENS BANDSTAND
ROYAL MARINES BAND

6.15pm - 6.55pm
EAST OVERCLIFF
ROYAL MARINES COMMANDO RECRUITING TEAM & ROYAL MARINES THE BEAT RETREAT

6.30pm - 9.00pm
LOWER GARDENS
CIRCUS WORKSHOP, AIR THEMED ROVING ENTERTAINMENT, FACE PAINTING AND PUNCH & JUDY

7.00pm - 9.00pm
LOWER GARDENS BANDSTAND
ARMY AIR CORPS BAND
6 PIECE ROCK POP COMBO

7.15pm - 8.35pm...

NIGHT AIR AEROBATICS
RR SPITFIRE, THE BLADES, O'BRIEN'S FLYING CIRCUS, SOLO TWISTER & THE RED DEVILS

7.00pm - 10.00pm
NIGHT AIR: BOSCOMBE STAGE
SOPHIE ELLIS-BEXTOR, THE STRUTS & JACK SAVORETTI
TICKET ONLY EVENT

8.30pm - 10.00pm
NIGHT AIR: BOURNEMOUTH STAGE
ABBA CHIQUE
TRIBUTE ACT

Don't forget... **FIREWORKS** near Bournemouth Pier at 10pm

AIR FESTIVAL TV SPONSORED BY **Mansell Homes**

Boscombe Pier: Corona Live Music Stage, presented by Wave 105 are ticketed only performance events.
Tickets on sale Saturday 26th July 2014. Subject to availability. See bhlivetickets.co.uk

bournemouthair.co.uk powered by Campbell Rowley

45

DAILY EVENT TIMETABLE

SUNDAY 31st

11.45am - 2.00pm...

SEAFRONT 11.25am - 11.40am
ROYAL MARINES COMMANDO RECRUITING TEAM

11.45am - 11.50am
FLYING SCHOLARSHIPS FOR DISABLED PEOPLE

12.10pm
AEROBATIC
RAF AEROBATIC TEAM THE RED ARROWS

BEACH
SEAFRONT IN FRONT OF RN & ARMY VILLAGE
ROYAL MARINES COMMANDO ASSAULT

AEROBATICS
THE BLADES EXTRA 300

FLYING DISPLAY
RAF BBMF MEMORIAL FLIGHT & CANADIAN LANCASTER

FLYING DISPLAY
RAF BBMF DAKOTA C-47

2.00pm - 3.10pm...

FLYING DISPLAY
ROYAL NAVY BLACK CATS
HELICOPTER DISPLAY TEAM

FLYING DISPLAY
ROYAL NAVY MERLIN HM1

FLYING DISPLAY
ARMY AIR CORPS LYNX

FLYING DISPLAY
B-17 SALLY-B FLYING FORTRESS

PARACHUTE DISPLAY TEAM
THE TIGERS

FLYING DISPLAY
ROYAL AIR FORCE TUTOR T1

FREE
UPDATED ONLINE AIR DISPLAY TIMETABLE WITH THIS BROCHURE

YOUR UNIQUE ACCESS CODE IS ENCLOSED

Bournemouth
BOROUGH COUNCIL
OFFICIAL EVENT

DAILY EVENT TIMETABLE

Listen to Air Festival Radio: 87.7FM

Commentary by George Bacon and Andy Robbins

BOURNEMOUTH AIR FESTIVAL

SUNDAY 31st

3.10pm - 4.15pm...

FLYING DISPLAY
ROYAL AIR FORCE TUCANO T1

FLYING DISPLAY
ROLLS ROYCE SPITFIRE

FLYING DISPLAY
ROYAL AIR FORCE CHINOOK

FLYING DISPLAY
SEA VIXEN

FLYING DISPLAY
HUNTER JET: MISS DEMEANOUR

FLYING DISPLAY
HERITAGE FLYPAST: CANBERRA, HUNTER JET & SEA VIXEN

4.15pm - 4.30pm...

FLYING DISPLAY
CANBERRA PR9

FLYING DISPLAY
ROYAL AIR FORCE TYPHOON FGR4

10am - 6pm
EVERYDAY:
PIER TO PIER &
EAST OVERCLIFF
STALLS & ATTRACTIONS

10am - 6pm
EVERYDAY:
NR EAST CLIFF
LIFT & BOSCOMBE
PIER
FUNFAIR

10am - 6pm
EVERYDAY: NR
EAST CLIFF LIFT
RN VILLAGE & ARMY
Feat: Commando
Weapons Dome, climbing
wall, Black Cats trailer

10am - 6pm
EVERYDAY:
PIER APPROACH
RAF VILLAGE
Feat: Full-size Chinook,
RAF Recruiting Team
and RAF Regiment 50 Squadron

AIR FESTIVAL TV SPONSORED BY
MansellHomes

bournemouthair.co.uk powered by Campbell Rowley

47

SPECTACULAR

NIGH

Corona Extra

The fun and entertainment doesn't stop with the last daytime flight, with dusk displays, live music, Beat Retreat performances, fireworks, street entertainment and the Royal Marines Commando Recruiting Team, the Air Festival is so much more than just an air show!

The incredible Night Air atmosphere, sponsored by Corona and supported by Wave105, official Night Air Radio Partner, will run from Boscombe to Bournemouth Pier through the Lower Gardens and into the town centre – get set for 3 fantastic nights of incredible entertainment, Thursday, Friday and Saturday.

Dusk Air Displays

This year the dynamic dusk air displays along the seafront will be bigger and better! Starting earlier

at 7.15pm Thursday, Friday and Saturday nights look out for Spitfire, Twister Team solo aircraft (G-ZWIP) with its swishing and swooping pyrotechnic displays alongside the awesome routines of O'Briens Flying Circus and back by popular demand the Red Devils' amazing night jumps complete with glow sticks and dazzling pyrotechnics. And, in a Night Air first, the Blades will be performing two very special sunset displays on Friday and Saturday.

East Overcliff

Literally kicking things off on the East Overcliff is the Royal Marines Commando Recruiting Team! Demonstrating their impressive fighting skills with specialists participating in unarmed combat, get ready to be impressed, just don't

practice this at home! The East Overcliff area is also home to the regal rhythms and visual splendour of the Beat Retreat, performed by HM Royal Marines Band. Dating back to the Middle Ages this is a historical must-see performance for everyone.

The Lower Gardens

Head to the Lower Gardens for some fantastic family Night Air entertainment. There will be circus workshops, face painting and hula hoop workshops...don't forget to look out for the air men entertainer's - one on stilts and the other on a tricycle! If that wasn't enough the bandstand will be hosting the Army Air Corp Band, their 6 piece rock/pop combo band will be playing some great tunes and favourites from 7-9pm

FAIR

Fireworks
OOOOH! Ahhh! The awesome Bournemouth Fireworks, sponsored by Mouchel, will be lighting up the night's sky Friday and Saturday night at 10pm with additional beach pyrotechnics on Thursday and Friday after the dusk displays.

Bournemouth Stage
There are some fantastic tribute bands taking to the Bournemouth music stage, check out the 'Silver Beatles' on Thursday, 'Bootleg Blondie' on Friday and 'Abba Chique' tribute act for Saturday. Concerts start approx 8.30pm

wave
105.2 FM
the south's best **variety** of hits

NIGHT AIR AT THE PIERS

TICKET ONLY EVENT

BOSCOMBE PIER LIVE MUSIC STAGE

Boscombe Pier Corona Live Music Stage, with Wave 105 – if you've already got your tickets you'll be in for a fantastic night of incredible live music, from chart toppers and up and coming acts, this is the place to be!

FRIDAY

Rixton

Hailing from Manchester, UK foursome Rixton are Jake Roche, Danny Wilkin, Charley Bagnall and Lewi Morgan. Their wealth of addictive pop, built on their own brand of song writing, instrumentation and pure vocal talent, which includes 'Me and My Broken Heart' and 'Make Out,' is sure to be a hit at this year's Wave105 Corona Music Stage!

Rizzle Kicks

Platinum selling Rizzle Kicks are back! Their two albums, "Stereo Typical" and "Roaring 20s" have established the duo as one of the most inspiring and refreshing acts to emerge from Britain in recent years and their brand new single "Tell Her" is released this summer. Set to be another awesome performance, 'Get down with the trumpets' and be part of the 'Lost Generation!'

Loveable Rouges

Loveable Rogues love Bournemouth and are also confirmed for Friday night! They have released their debut album 'This and That', the perfect summer soundtrack earlier this month and will be performing some of their original, fun and organic sounds, there's no denying, these boy are pretty loveable.

Alexa Goddard

Alexa Goddard is set to rock the pop scene in 2014! Her debut single Marilyn' has wowed her fans with its irresistible hook and sing-a-long chorus. Catch this up and coming artist.

Corona Extra

wave 105.2 FM

the south's best **variety** of hits

For tickets visit: bhlivetickets.co.uk • For tickets visit: bhlivetickets.co.uk • For ticke...

SATURDAY

Sophie Ellis Bextor...

Having spent over a decade finessing her pop vision over four albums – in the process selling over five million records, Sophie Ellis-Bextor is back with her fifth album 'Wanderlust'. Career highs include Groovejet ('If This Ain't Love'), 'Murder On The Dancefloor', 'Take Me Home' and 'Catch You' and we can't wait to welcome her to Bournemouth!

The Struts...

They've just supported The Rolling Stones and Black Sabbath, played the Isle of Wight Fstival (and many others across the course of the summer), and are tipped for big things, with the lead singer drawing many comparisons to Jagger and Freddie Mercury – you've seen them here first!

Friday and Saturday night at Boscombe Pier stage are both events where tickets would have been purchased in advance - bhlivetickets.co.uk no ticket no entry. Acts and times are correct at the time of going to print and may be subject to change.

ON THE **GROUND** HIGHLIGHTS

With so much going on from 10am here are some of the attractions...

Zone 1 Transformers with Optimus Prime, 'The Free From Tour' healthy alternative foods, Ashai Koh Lounge, Little Tikes, Tank Heroes and Night Air Corona Music Stage with Wave105.

Zone 2 Check out the Royal Marine beach assaults, Wave105, Air Festival Hospitality, BBC Radio Solent, Army and Royal Navy and Royal Marines.

Zone 3 Haribo, Samsung, Barny, Night Air Corona live music stage, Air Festival merchandise.

Zone 4 Night Air entertainment in the Lower gardens and Pier Approach – RAF Village, Avon, Nintendo.

Zone 5 Westbeach marquee.

Zone 6 East Overcliff – Beat Retreat, trading and food area, Falconry UK, Royal Marines Commando Recruiting Team.

SEE SITE MAP ON PAGE 42 & 43 for approximate locations.

Flying Scholarships For Disabled People will be taking to the skies everyday before the flying displays start.

Stay sun safe! Wear a hat, sunglasses, apply suncream and drink plenty of water!

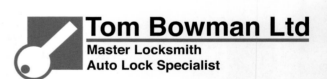

MEET THE PILOTS

Vulcan

Martin Withers joined the RAF in 1968 and after training was posted to the Vulcan. He later became a qualified flying instructor.

He flew in the Falklands War and for his part in bombing the runway at Port Stanley he was awarded the Distinguished Flying Cross.

After the war Martin became Deputy Chief Instructor (DCI) and OC Standards Squadron, before leaving to become an airline pilot.

The Blades

With over 30,000 hours of flying between them, The Blades are amongst the most experienced display pilots in the UK. Add to the fact that all are former RAF fast-jet pilots and former Red Arrows its little wonder their air display is renowned world-wide.

The team is made up of Leader & Blade 1 Mark Cutmore, Andy Offer (OBE) Director and Blade 2, Chris Carder also flies as Blade 2 as does founding member Myles Garland. Ian Smith Blade 3; who has over 6,000 flying hours across a range of aircraft and Andy Evans Blade 4 who is a qualified Flying Instructor.

RAF BBMF Bomber Pilots

Flight Lieutenant Tim Dunlop is responsible for training and standardization of the 'Bomber' pilots and crew; this is his sixth season with BBMF. Flight Lieutenant Roger Nichols (Dakota and Lancaster captain and Flying Instructor) and Flight Lieutenant Loz Rushmere (Dakota and Lancaster captain) joined the RAF in 1988, this is their eighth season with the BBMF. Flight Lieutenant Seb Davey is Dakota Captain and Lancaster co-pilot and has flown with the BBMF since 2011. Flight Lieutenant Neil Farrell joined the RAF in 1996 this is his first season with the Flight. Flight Lieutenant Matt Jenkinson is this season's Dakota Captain.

RAF Typhoon

Flight Lieutenant Noel Rees was born in Southampton and grew up on the south coast in Hampshire. Noel joined the RAF in 2002. He has taken part in multiple overseas deployments and exercises to the South Atlantic, USA and Europe and completed the Tactical Leadership Programme (TLP). Noel was posted to the Typhoon Force in 2011 and after completing the Operational Conversion Unit (OCU) he remained on 29(R) Squadron as a Typhoon Qualified Flying Instructor (QFI). Noel has trained many of the front line Typhoon pilots, is an Electronic Warfare Instructor (EWI) and contributes to RAF Coningsby's primary task of Quick Reaction Alert.

Canadian Lancaster

Don Schofield was born in England so this trip will be like coming home for him. After moving to Canada in the fifties, he joined the RCAF where he flew the CF-100, CF-101 Voodoo, Caribou and Hercules. Don then moved over to Air Canada where he flew pretty much everything they owned and retired from the B747 and Airbus A330/340.

Don started flying the Canadian Warplane Heritage Museum's Lancaster shortly after completion of its restoration in 1988 and is now the current highest time Lancaster pilot in the world with almost 750 hours.

RN Black Cats

Wildcat: Lt Cdr Gary McCall.
After gaining his pilot wings on the Lynx in 2000 he has operated from RN Frigates and Destroyers across the globe. A Qualified Helicopter Instructor, a Flight Commander and Training Officer on the Lynx Force, responsible for flying standards across the Lynx Wildcat Maritime Force.

The Lynx: Lt Ian Houlston.
Flown by life-long Poole & Bournemouth resident, Ian has served in Iraq and Caribbean counter-narcotic operations. He has trained in UK security operations and provided airborne defence for the London Olympics. A Qualified Helicopter Instructor, Ian is Black Cat Team Leader.

RAF **TUTOR**

raf.mod.uk/tutordisplayteam 🌐

This is where it all begins for RAF and Royal Navy pilots. Whether you want to fly in the Red Arrows or pilot the Typhoon – or both – everyone starts behind the controls of a Grob Tutor.

The Grob 115E Tutor was built and equipped especially for the RAF in Mattsies, Germany, between 1999 and 2002.

It is 96 per cent carbon fibre, of Semi-monocoque construction and is fully aerobatic. Powered by a single 180hp Textron-Lycoming engine, it can accommodate two crew members sitting side by side and is used for elementary flying training, university air squadron and air experience flying by cadets.

It now has hundreds of thousands of flying hours with the RAF under its belt and will remain in the service for some time to come.

Appearance supported by
BH Live
Leisure, International Venues & Events

RAF **TUCANO**

raf.mod.uk/tucanodisplayteam 🌐

It is to tie in with this year's team charities, which are the Royal British Legion, the Royal Air Forces Association and the Jon Egging Trust.

The aircraft itself is step two in RAF and Navy pilot training. The Tucano T1 is a modified version of the Brazilian Embraer EMB-312 Tucano aircraft and was built under licence by Shorts of Belfast.

The tandem cockpit layout of the Tucano prepares the student pilot for progression onto the Hawk T1/T2 advanced flying trainer and then onto fast-jet aircraft on the front line.

Having sported a desert camouflage paint job last year in honour of Spitfire aircraft operated by No 72 Squadron in 1943, this year the Tucano will sport a scheme that includes poppies and the words 'Lest We Forget'.

It replaced the Jet Provost in RAF service and the Tucano is operated primarily from No 1 Flying Training School at RAF Linton-On-Ouse, to provide basic fast jet flying training to RAF and RN student pilots and basic WSO (Weapon Systems Officer) training to all potential RAF pilots.

Appearance supported by
BH Live
Leisure, International Venues & Events

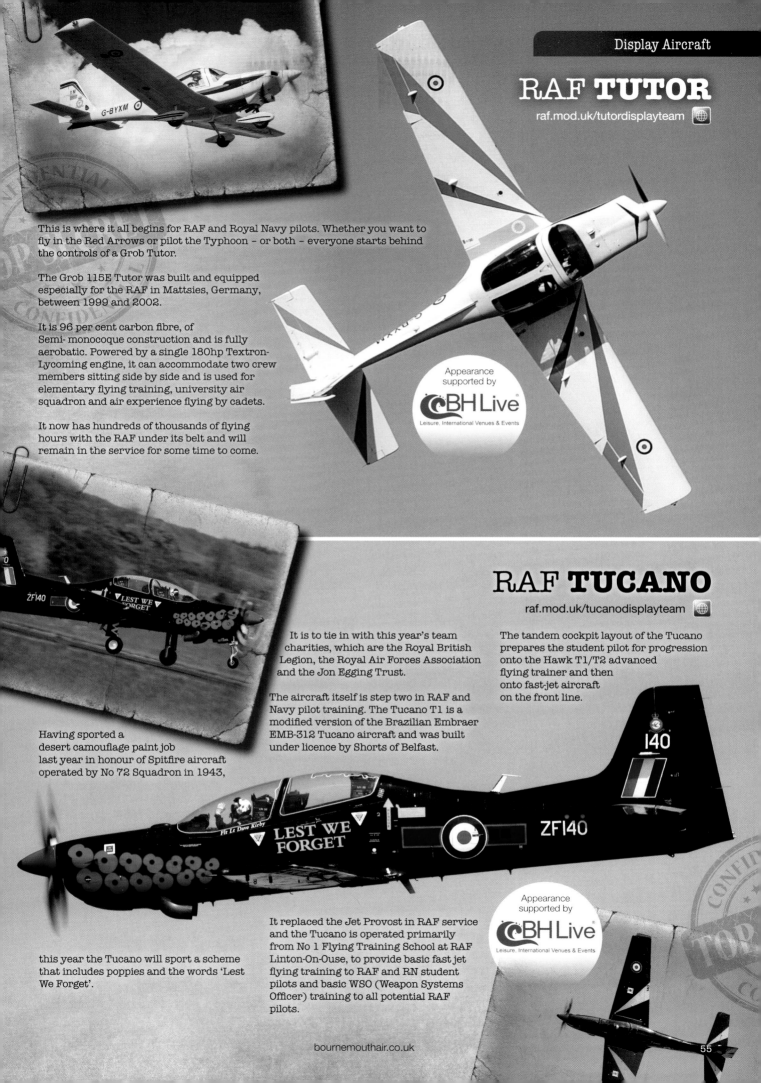

BUILD A WORLD CLASS CAREER.

HAVE A WORLD CLASS LIFE.

Find out more about opportunities in Bournemouth

It may surprise you to know that Bournemouth is a key location in our global organisation. In fact, it has the largest technology and operations team in Europe, with more than 4,000 people supporting activities in more than 40 countries. And it offers global exposure and mobility, as well as exceptional career development opportunities.

But what really sets Bournemouth apart is the life that goes along with it. Enjoy our beautiful surroundings, visit worldclass restaurants and cycle through the New Forest. All of it makes living here something truly special. Apply today and discover the possibilities.

We want what you're made of.

jpmorgan.com/careers

J.P.Morgan

THE **BLADES**

theblades.com 🌐

For pure aerobatic breathtaking thrills, it's hard to beat The Blades.

The team, which fly Extra 300 LP and the latest 330 SC aircraft, is made up of some very experienced pilots – all of which are former members of the Red Arrows.

The Blades have quickly become one of the hottest on the circuit, having formed only seven years ago.

Spectacular mid-air acrobatics come as standard and the two-seat Extras can turn harder and faster than anyone else. They also lay claim to being the only aerobatic airline in the world – the two-seater planes can be booked out for passenger flights.

So get ready for an incredible array of gyroscopic tumbles, close formation manoeuvres and opposition passes.

The Blades are among the world's best aerobatic pilots, flying the ultimate in high-performance piston aircraft.

The Blades have flown hundreds of displays in front of more than 18 million people and carried in excess of 1,000 corporate flying event passengers.

army.mod.uk/equipment 🌐 # ARMY SOLO **LYNX**

Not to be outdone by those Royal Navy and RAF boys and girls, the army is having its go in the sky with the solo Lynx display. The Lynx has been used extensively within the Army Air Corps for a wide variety of roles and tasks.

It is predominantly a battlefield utility helicopter, although it has been used for both anti-tank and reconnaissance operations.

The addition of door gunners has allowed the Lynx to operate in the very close air support role in Iraq and Afghanistan.

The Lynx is the fastest helicopter in the world and, thanks to its semi-rigid titanium rotor head, it is also superbly manoeuvrable.

This makes it the centrepiece of Army Aviation display flying. It is fitted with a more advanced communication system, improved surveillance equipment and the M3M Machine Gun - a 0.50" calibre weapon, capable of firing over 850 rounds a minute. The model flying at Bournemouth will be the AH7 and it is the final display season for the Lynx with the Army Air Corps.

Appearance supported by

THE **CUMBERLAND**
HOTEL BAR BRASSERIE

Come home
to Weymouth
Your new holiday home awaits you at Littlesea

Littlesea Holiday Park

Lodges start from only **£129,995***

Plus caravan holiday homes from just **£16,995***

Spacious bedrooms & master en-suite

Modern open plan living space

High specification fitted kitchens

We've got it all!

- New 2014 Pebbles Owners lounge and bar
- Heated indoor and outdoor pools
- 2 Tennis courts
- Adventure golf
- Kids' clubs for all ages

- Choice of bars and restaurants
- Family entertainment
- Owners' events and benefits
- Sea views
- Wide range of affordable holiday homes

For more information or to book a viewing

call: **07779 277 659** visit: **littleseaholidaypark.co.uk**

Littlesea Holiday Park, Lynch Lane, Weymouth, Dorset, DT4 9DT

AWAITING YOUR INSTRUCTIONS

**24 RESIDENTIAL OFFICES, 18 LETTINGS OFFICES
& 4 COMMERCIAL OFFICES**

Covering Dorset, Hampshire & Wiltshire.

goadsby.com

ROYAL AIR FORCE **FALCONS**
PARACHUTE DISPLAY TEAM

Widely recognised as the UK's premier military parachute display team, the Falcons, based at RAF Brize Norton, Oxfordshire, display at venues all over Britain and Europe throughout the year.

The Royal Air Force is responsible for training and supporting all UK Airborne Forces.

As well as providing a distinctive demonstration of freefall and canopy skills during the display seasons each Falcons Team member undertakes continual advanced training as Parachute Jumping Instructors in preparation for future employment in support of the Parachute Regiment, the Royal Marines and other specialist units.

raf.mod.uk/falcons

RED DEVILS
PARACHUTE REGIMENT
FREEFALL TEAM

reddevilsonline.com

The Parachute Regiment Freefall Team 'The Red Devils' is the official parachute display team of both The Parachute Regiment (The Paras) and the British Army.

The team's role is to promote both the Parachute Regiment and the British Army in support of recruitment and is currently manned by 12 serving soldiers from The Parachute Regiment's three full-time Battalions: 1, 2 & 3 PARA.

Every member of the team has served a minimum of three years in The Parachute Regiment Battalion and has taken part in at least one operational tour of duty in either: The Falkland Islands, Northern Ireland, Kosovo, Sierra Leone, Afghanistan and/or Iraq.

Disclaimer: Both Display Teams are highly qualified and capable, however there is always the possibility of an unforeseen accident or incident. Spectators who watch the display do so at their own risk with regard to what they witness. No related spectator claims will be supported.

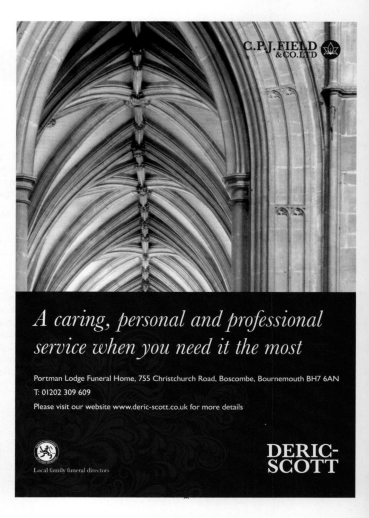

B-17 FLYING FORTRESS
SALLY-B

sallyb.org.uk

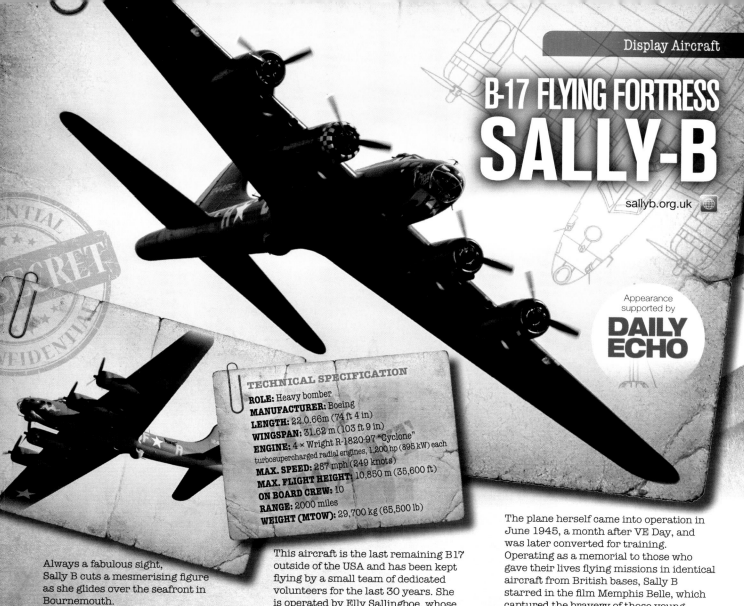

TECHNICAL SPECIFICATION

ROLE: Heavy bomber
MANUFACTURER: Boeing
LENGTH: 22.0.66m (74 ft 4 in)
WINGSPAN: 31.62 m (103 ft 9 in)
ENGINE: 4 × Wright R-1820-97 "Cyclone" turbosupercharged radial engines, 1,200 hp (895 kW) each
MAX. SPEED: 287 mph (249 knots)
MAX. FLIGHT HEIGHT: 10,850 m (35,600 ft)
ON BOARD CREW: 10
RANGE: 2000 miles
WEIGHT (MTOW): 29,700 kg (65,500 lb)

Always a fabulous sight, Sally B cuts a mesmerising figure as she glides over the seafront in Bournemouth.

When she does so, it's hard not to think of the brave American airman who flew daring bombing missions from Britain to Germany during WWII.

This aircraft is the last remaining B17 outside of the USA and has been kept flying by a small team of dedicated volunteers for the last 30 years. She is operated by Elly Sallingboe, whose long-time companion, the late Ted White, brought the bomber to the UK and named it after Elly. B17 Preservation keeps her in the air, with the help of the Sally B Supporters Club.

The plane herself came into operation in June 1945, a month after VE Day, and was later converted for training. Operating as a memorial to those who gave their lives flying missions in identical aircraft from British bases, Sally B starred in the film Memphis Belle, which captured the bravery of those young air crews. Keeping her in the air is a mission in itself - it is down to volunteers, members, donations, sponsorship and souvenir sales, a remarkable achievement over several decades.

ROLLS ROYCE SPITFIRE

Supermarine Spitfire PR Mk XIX-PS853 was built in Southampton and delivered to the central Photographic Reconnaissance Unit at RAF Benson on January 13, 1945.

Her career has seen her join Squadrons in Europe, 6 MU (Maintenance Unit), THUM Flight (Temperature and Humidity Flight) the Battle of Britain Memorial Flight, 32 MU, Station Flight at Biggin Hill and North Weald, and Central Fighter Establishment.

She was struck off charge on May 1, 1958 and became West Rayham's gate guardian until 1961 when she was restored to flying condition. In 1964 she transferred to the Battle of Britain Memorial Flight at RAF Coltishall and in 1967 starred in the film 'Battle of Britain', returning to the Flight once filming was completed.

In 1995 she was sold with registration G-MXIX early in 1995 but was put back up for sale in 1996 when Rolls Royce Heritage Department purchased her and her registration became G-RRGN (short for Rolls Royce Griffin, the engine that powers this particular mark of Spitfire).

Summer 2015
ON SALE NOW

Visit your local branch for great offers including:

- **Low deposits**
- **Departures from Bournemouth Airport**

TURKISH RIVIERA
ESCORTED TOUR
02, 09 April 2015 | 7 nights
Flying from Bournemouth

Prices start
from only
£249
Per person

BATH TRAVEL

For more details visit your local Bath Travel branch or call:
01202 238844

TWISTER AEROBATIC SOLO

twister-aerobatics.co.uk

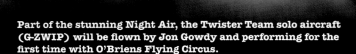

Part of the stunning Night Air, the Twister Team solo aircraft (G-ZWIP) will be flown by Jon Gowdy and performing for the first time with O'Briens Flying Circus.

Watch him take to the skies in a glittering and sparkling performance on Thursday, Friday and Saturday night.

See pilot Jon at his best - flying challenging, precision aerobatics. The Twister display is designed to get the perfect performance from the aircraft. The smoke system is the best in its class, with a safe purified baby oil derivative injected into the exhaust to create the dense white smoke.

The aerobatic figures are generally smooth and flowing as the Twister constantly manoeuvres along the crowd line, and with every formation change, break and formation join, the smoke shows the flight history.

The SA1100 Silence Twister started life as a world-beating radio-controlled aerobatic machine simply known as the Twister. It had been developed by Matthias and Thomas Strieker in Germany and was so successful that they decided to build a 'real' version of the model. The Silence Twister uses a honeycomb core. While more expensive, it makes the structure lightweight and very tough.

Always worth watching, O'Brien's Flying Circus is back at Bournemouth this year.

This is likely to be one of the craziest displays this year. In fact, it definitely will be.

O'Brien's Flying Circus normally headlines with a routine that renowned pilot and commentator Brendan O'Brien developed during the late 1980s and involves a Cub landing on the back of a mobile platform.

With Brendan at the controls things become increasingly entertaining as the Cub cavorts around the airfield with a zany flying routine.

At Bournemouth – where the sea suffers from a distinct lack of tarmac – crowds can expect a display of crazy flying instead – with a surprise or two thrown in.

The plane used to display is a Piper J-3 Cub, an iconic aircraft. 19,073 J-3 Cubs were sold between 1938 and 1947, the majority of them for military roles. Post-war the aircraft proved popular with the civilian market for flying training and touring.

G-BPCF is a clipped wing Piper J3-65 Cub. The wings are clipped at the centre of the span by 4ft per wing which increases the roll performance.

Combined with a superb environmentally-friendly smoke system, "CF" is the perfect barnstorming machine!

O'BRIEN'S FLYING CIRCUS

obriensflyingcircus.com

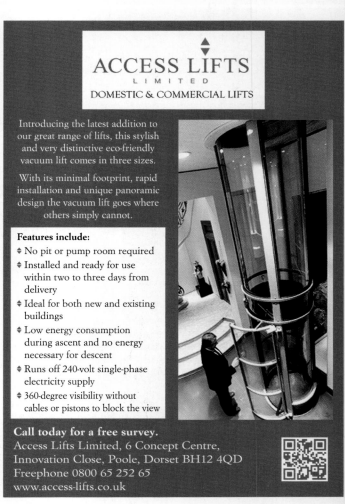

MEET THE PILOTS

RAF BBMF Fighter Pilots

The BBMF Fighter Pilots are: Group Captain Johnny Stringer this is his second season with the Flight. Wing Commander Justin Helliwell took command of Operations Wing at RAF Coningsby in June 2013, this is his first season with the Flight. Ex-Red Arrow pilot Squadron Leader Dunc Mason joined the BBMF in 2009 and has flown all of the fighters for the last six years. Squadron Leader Andy Millikin was educated at Southampton University, he is a third generation aviator. Flight Lieutenant Antony Parkinson, joined the RAF at 18 he was the first pilot to gain 1000 hours flying the RAF"s latest fighter the Euro Fighter Typhoon.

Brendan O'Brien

Brendan has over thirteen thousand hours experience on over three hundred types of aircraft and holds a licence to fly every kind of flying machine. He holds in excess of two hundred aviation world records ratified by the FAI in Paris. He is a CAA display authorisation holder/examiner, test pilot and medallist of the Royal Aero Club and has flown on every continent in the world including Antarctica. Brendan also trained as a civil and military parachutist and has taken part in several international para-military expeditions including the famous Trans Americas crossing of the infamous Darien Gap.

Canberra PR9

Midair Squadron Chief Pilot - Flight Lieutenant Mike Leckey
Born in Belfast in 1965, Mike Leckey was educated at the Belfast Royal Academy and Queen's University in Belfast. In 1988 Mike joined the Royal Air Force and on completion of flying training in 1991, he was posted to fly the Canberra T17 on 360 Sqn. He remained here until 1994 when the Squadron was disbanded. Mike is currently a Leadership Instructor at the RAF College, Cranwell. He has 5500hrs flying experience, of which 2700hrs are on the Canberra. He will fly the Squadron's Canberra PR9 alongside his duties at Cranwell.

Tom Lackey

Tom's first Wingwalk was at the age of 80, having just lost his wife he decided that sitting at home and moping was not for him! He is now 95 and is a Guinness book of records holder for the following; Aged 85 the oldest person to do a Loop the loop on the Wing. In 2009 he crossed the Channel from Calais to a field in Dover to co-inside with Bleroit taking the same route 100 years before. In 2011 he did a double crossing of the same route! In 2013 he went from Castle Kennedy in Scotland to Londonderry, NI ,on the Wing a total flight time of 1hour and 21 minutes. On May 22nd 2014 he went from Lands End to St Mary's Scilly Isles 30 miles across the water on his 95th Birthday!

Miss Demeanour

This year Jonathon Whaley will be flying the Sea Vixen and Miss Demeanour will be flown by either Mark Southern or Patrick Tuit.

Mark is an ex military RAF fast jet pilot. Recently flying the Tornado F3 he is a qualified flying instructor on the Jet Provost amassing over 6,000 hours and unbelievably has spent over two years of his life in the air. He now flies the 757 and 767 as a training captain for Thomas Cook.

Patrick Tuit is a Hunter pilot, he flies the historic Dutch Hunter, owned by the Dutch Hawker Hunter Foundation. He was also a former RNLAF F-16 Display Pilot (1997-1998).

RAF BBMF Dakota

Flight Lieutenant Matt Jenkinson
Matt joined the RAF in 1999 and after Initial Officer Training he followed the fast-jet training stream until the GR4 OCU, at which point it became apparent his strengths lay in the multi engine environment! Following a brief conversion course in 2005, Matt was posted to the Special Forces Flight on 47 Squadron flying the C-130K, which saw him operating the Hercules in the Tactical role across the globe. At the start of this year, Matt was posted to 206(R) Heavy Aircraft Test & Evaluation Squadron at MoD Boscombe Down as the C-17 Evaluator Pilot where he will help to develop the C-17's future capabilities.

ROYAL NAVY
BLACK CATS
HELICOPTER DISPLAY TEAM

facebook.com/RoyalNavyBlackCats

THE BLACK CATS
ROYAL NAVY HELICOPTER DISPLAY TEAM

WILDCAT TECHNICAL SPEC.

ROLE: Multi-purpose military helicopter
MANUFACTURER: Agusta Westland
LENGTH: 15.24 m (50 ft 0 in)
MAIN ROTOR DIAMETER: 12.8 m (42 ft 0 in)
ENGINE: 2 × LHTEC CTS800-4N turboshaft, 1,015 kW (1,361 hp) each
MAX. SPEED: 181mph (157 knots)
ON BOARD CREW: Two
RANGE: 483 miles
WEIGHT (MTOW): 6,000 kg (13,228 lb)

The Black Cats are the display team of the Royal Navy and have become a regular fixture at Bournemouth Air Festival.

Things will be a bit different this year, as the team will be made up of the Lynx Mk8 that has served the team so well over the years, joined by the latest version, the AW159 Wildcat HMA MK2.

The Wildcat is the latest generation of multi role helicopter specifically procured to operate from the Frigates and Destroyers of the Royal Navy.

For those that want to see helicopters in positions and angles that don't look like they should be possible, the Black Cats are for you. They are out to show that anything fixed-wing aircraft pilots can do, they can do too.

The display will include all kinds of moves, including formation flying, nose-overs and the carousel.

For the nose-over, the helicopter tilts 90 degrees so the nose is facing the ground, while the carousel sees two helicopters bring themselves nose to nose and 'dance' with each other in the air.
The manoeuvres have been linked

together to focus on achieving a dynamic, vertical and crowd-centred routine perfect for the venues they will be displaying at around the country.

The Westland Lynx is used for a variety of roles in the Royal Navy and is powered by two Rolls Royce Gem engines, while composite main rotor blades give the MK8 variant a top speed of 174 Kts.

Operationally, the Lynx is an effective search asset and weapons platform. It is able to deploy up to four anti-ship Sea Skua missiles and can take up to two Sting Ray torpedoes or depth charges.

It can also be fitted with the M3M 0.5" Heavy Machine Gun for use against smaller surface targets.

Electronically it boasts the Seaspray radar and Orange Crop Electronic Support Measure for surface search.

The Wildcat, which is 15m in length, has a range of 420 nautical miles and a top speed of 157 knots. Its armament includes forward-firing CRV7 rockets and machine guns, a Pintle mounted machine gun and air-to-surface Missile systems.

LOW FARES
FROM BOURNEMOUTH

ALICANTE

CHANIA

FUERTEVENTURA

MALAGA

TENERIFE

 ALLOCATED SEATING   FREE 2ND CABIN BAG

 RYANAIR
LOW FARES. MADE SIMPLE.

RYANAIR.COM

royalnavy.mod.uk 🌐 ROYAL MARINES

THE BEAT RETREAT

The ceremony of Beating Retreat has its origins in the battles of the Middle Ages when, at dusk, a drummer boy was sent along the ranks of the infantry to beat retreat. In the seventeenth century 'Retreat' and 'Tattoo' were embellished by the addition of files playing martial airs.

During the eighteenth century, bands were added, often giving a torchlight display as an entertainment for the garrison. In the Royal Marines, the ceremony gained importance during the 1930s, when the Divisional bands accompanied Naval visits to foreign ports.

Today's ceremony begins with the band playing traditional tunes as it marches and counter marches leading to the Drum Beatings.

The band then moves to a central position for the Finale, which includes an evening hymn and the performance of sunset.
Did you know... The Wolsey pattern white helmet became the ceremonial headdress of the Royal Marines in 1912. It has to be painted regularly to keep it perfectly white... The Drum Major's Ceremonial Staff is used to give marching signals to the band. The silver ball on top of the staff is a 3D version of the Royal Marines emblem.

When: Thursday, Friday and Saturday evening
Times: 6.15pm: Royal Marines Commmando Recruiting Team
6.30pm: Beat Retreat, performed by The Band of HM Royal Marines CTCRM
Where: East Overcliff Drive, on the green area at the junction of Manor Road and East Overcliff Drive

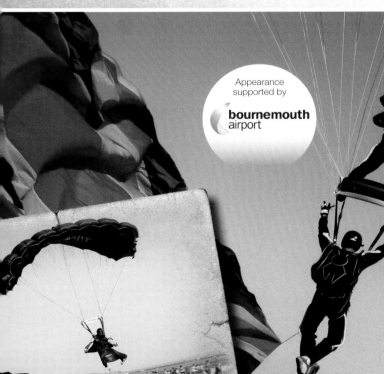

THE TIGERS

thetigersfft.co.uk 🌐

Appearance supported by **bournemouth airport**

The Tigers are ready to roar for another year in Bournemouth. They made their debut in 2010 and are the Princess of Wales's Royal Regiment's Parachute Display Team.

All experienced army parachutists, The Tigers will certainly impress as they drop from the sky in amazing formations with smoke trailing and flags flying.

The team has now been around for more than 20 years and has established itself as one of the top parachute display teams in the UK.

This year the team are Team Commander Captain Ian Wicks, team leader Cpl Frank Millerick, Cpl SI Geraing, LCpl Rodger Smith, Pte Will Forbes, Pte Gary Chapman, Pte Jake Manwaring and not forgetting Team Founder, Field Marshal Tigger The Tiger.

ROYAL NAVY VILLAGE

Situated at the centre of the Festival site the Royal Navy and Royal Marines are back with their joint interactive village area.

Bringing ground assets, attractions, weapons dome and hands on action this is an essential insight into life in the Royal Navy and Royal Marines.

Offshore Raiding Craft (ORC)

The Offshore Raiding Craft is a fast and versatile craft that can carry twelve Royal Marines Commandos and has a forward gun mount for a General Purpose Machine Gun (GPMG).

The Band of HM Royal Marines (CTCRM)

Lead by Captain Huw Williams, Director of Music, watch the band perform the historic Beat Retreat on the East Overcliff Thursday, Friday and Saturday, after the unarmed combat display at 6.15pm.

Royal Flight Auxillary (RFA)

A career in the Royal Fleet Auxiliary offers all the opportunities for travel, adventure and responsibility that go with a life at sea – find out more and speak to a member of the RFA.

Royal Naval Association Representative

A family for current and former Naval Service personnel, relatives and supporters of our country's Royal Navy the RNA promote unity, loyalty, patriotism and comradeship.

Royal Navy Ships

At sea will be a 6 ship flotilla, which includes the French Navy's FS Sagittaire alongside the RFA Argus, HMS Westminster, open to visitors, and HMS Mersey. The Patrol Vessels HMS Puncher and HMS Smiter complete the force.

Ship open to visitors timetable*
You can visit HMS Westminster Friday, Saturday and Sunday. The transfer boats take 90 people per hour from 10.30am outside the flying display times – there will be no access to the ships during display times.

ROYAL NAVY VILLAGE

Sea Cadets

As a Sea Cadet you can go to sea, learn to sail and go adventure training – if you're interested in finding out more, have a chat with members of the UKs largest maritime youth charity, who will be there to chat to. If you're aged 8-18 and interested in all things naval this is perfect!

Royal Navy Royal Marines Charity

One of this year's nominated Air Festival's official charities, find out how they make a difference.

RN Presentation Team

Ideal opportunity to see how your Royal Navy operates across a spectrum of missions from counter-narcotics and anti-terrorism to Defence Diplomacy, disaster relief and peace keeping through crisis management all the way up to high intensity conflict.

Royal Naval Reserve HMS King Alfred

Members from the HMS King Alfred unit will be on hand to chat about their role in supporting the regular Royal Navy and how to join the Reserve Unit.

The Royal Marines

The Royal Marines are the amphibious infantry of the Royal Navy. They will be playing a big role at the Royal Navy Village, with the Weapons Display Dome, amphibious demonstrations and don't forget to watch them perform their unarmed combat displays on the East Overcliff on Thursday, Friday and Saturday at 6.15pm.

Black Cats trailer

See them in the sky and meet them in the village! Members of the ground crew will be there daily and pilots also visiting, times to be confirmed, simply ask on the day.

Fly Navy Heritage Trust

Your chance to purchase items in support of the Navy's heritage aircraft.

Mobile Recruiting

Are you interested in a career in the Royal Marines or Royal Navy? Visit the recruitment vehicle for all the advice and information you need.

Beach demonstrations

Don't miss the amphibious beach assault on Saturday and Sunday (12.45 - 1.15pm) which features Landing Craft, Viking All Terrain Vehicles, helicopter, sea boats, and of course the Royal Marines.

*Tickets are available from the Recruiting Stand in the RN Village. Please note tickets will be allocated on a first come first served basis and visitors will be advised to show their Air Festival charity wristbands or make a £1 donation to guarantee admission.

SHOREFIELD
HOLIDAYS LIMITED

Self Catering & Touring Holidays
In Hampshire & Dorset on the beautiful South Coast

Call or go Online for prices!

We offer the perfect settings to relax and explore the beautiful countryside and glorious beaches. With a variety of holiday accommodation in fully equipped chalets, caravans, lodges and bungalows, some with hot tubs, as well as touring and camping pitches, there is something for everyone. The parks have access to extensive leisure facilities and activities, whichever you choose you can be assured of a warm welcome.

WWW.SHOREFIELD.CO.UK
call us: **01590 648331** *email us:* **holidays@shorefield.co.uk**

AIRSHOW14

ARMY VILLAGE

The Army Village is located on Bournemouth seafront, next to the Royal Navy village, between the Piers and it's the perfect place to come and discover more about the Army, the impressive equipment they use and to find out what life is like as a soldier.

LAND VEHICLES....

Challenger 2 Main Battle Tank
Located on the seafront in the Army village will be a Challenger 2 (CR2), the British Army's main battle tank – this is a great opportunity to see a tank close up.

Jackal 2
Jackal 2 is a high mobility weapons platform, with rapid movement across varying terrain it is designed to protect personnel against roadside explosions and mine attacks.

CVRT Scimitar Armoured Reconnaissance Vehicle
Used by reconnaissance regiments of the Royal Armoured Corps and 'recce' elements of the armoured infantry, the Scimitar is useful where terrain is hostile and movement difficult.

Trojan Armoured Vehicle
Designed to open routes through complex battlefield obstacles and clear a path through minefields, standard equipment includes a dozer blade, mine plough and an excavator arm. That's not forgetting the Combat Support Boat, Terex Crane and 15t truck!

HELICOPTERS...

Check out a static Apache flight simulator and demo Gazelle.

ARMOURY...

The AS90
AS90 is a 155mm self-propelled gun that equips regiments of the Royal Horse Artillery and Royal Artillery and can fire a 38Kg shell over 24 kilometres.

L118 light gun
The versatile 105mm light gun, battle proven over many years and used by the parachute and commando artillery regiments of the British Army.

Starstreak High Velocity Missile (HVM)
Designed to counter threats from very high performance, low-flying aircraft and fast 'pop up' strikes the HVM travels at more than three times the speed of sound.
There's also set to be plenty more equipment on display including the Desert Hawk UAV, Small Arms, and Mine Detecting equipment.

Music
The Band of the Army Air Corps will be performing everyday 7.00pm Thursday, Friday and Saturday evening in the Lower Gardens Bandstand, showing the range of skills needed by modern military musicians.

The Army is always recruiting If you want to find out more about a career in the Army or Army Reserves then recruiting team will be there to talk to or search armyjobs online.

AIRCRAFT FACTS

Miss Demeanour

Role: ....Fighter and ground attack aircraft
Manufacturer: ....Hawker Siddeley
Length: 14m (45ft 11ins)
Wingspan: 10.26m (33ft 8ins)
Height: 4.01m (13ft 2ins)
Engine: ....1 x Rolls-Royce Avon 207 turbojet
Max. Speed: ....715mph (621 knots)
Service ceiling: 50,000ft (15,240m)
Aircrew: 1
Range: ....445 miles
Empty weight: ....6,405 kg (14,120 lb)

Sea Vixen

Role: ....Carrier-based fighter
Manufacturer: ....De Havilland
Length: 16.76m (55ft)
Wingspan: ....15.24 m (50ft)
Height: 3.28m (10ft 9ins)
Engine: ....2x Rolls Royce Avon Mk208 turbojets
Max. Speed: ....690mph (600 knots) at sea level
Service ceiling: 45,000ft (13,716m)
Aircrew: 2
Range: ....790 miles
Empty weight: ....19,050kg (42,000 lbs)

Army Lynx

Role: ....Multi-purpose military helicopter
Manufacturer: ....Agusta Westland
Length: 13.4m (43ft, 11ins)
Main Rotor Diameter: 12.8m (41ft, 11ins)
Engine: ....2 x Rolls-Royce Gem turboshaft, 835 kW (1,120 shp) each
Max. Speed: ....207mph (180 knots)
Aircrew: 2
Range: ....328 miles
Weight (MTOW): ....5,330 kg (11,750 lb)

BBMF Spitfire

Role: ....Multi-role fighter
Manufacturer: ....Supermarine
First flight: ....March 1936
Aircrew: 1
Height: 4m (13ft 1.5ins)
Length: 9.12m (29ft 11ins)
Wingspan: 11.25m (36ft 11ins)
Empty weight: 2,309kg (5,090lbs)
Engine: ......Rolls Royce Merlin 45 supercharged V12
Max speed: ....362mph (315 knots)
Range: ....410 miles
Max altitude: 35,000ft (10,668m)

BBMF Hurricane

Role: ....Multi-role fighter
Manufacturer: ....Hawker Aircraft
First flight: ....November 1935
Aircrew: 1
Height: 4m (13ft 1.5ins)
Length: 9.84m (32ft 3.5ins)
Wingspan: 12.19m (40ft)
Empty weight: 2,605kg (5,743lbs)
Engine: ......Rolls Royce Merlin XX liquid-cooled V12
Max speed: ....340mph (295 knots)
Range: ....600 miles
Max altitude: 36,000ft (10,970m)

O'Brien Flying Circus

Manufacturer: ....Piper
Type: ....J3C-65 Cub (Modified)
Year Built: 1940
Aircrew: 1
Power: 100hp
Wingspan: 8.61m (28ft 3ins)
Max. take-off weight: 499kg (1100lbs)
Engine: ....Continental O-200-A (McCauley 1A90)
Max speed: ....87mph (75.5 knots)
Special effects: ....Smoke sytem
....Lights
....Lasers
..................................Pyrotechnics

ROYAL AIR FORCE VILLAGE

Located at The Waterfront at Pier Approach, come and find out about life in the Armed Forces first hand from members of the RAF – the perfect opportunity if you're interested in kick starting your RAF career.

Chinook mock-up
Full size mock-up of the work horse of the RAF; get inside this fully interactive facsimile – which, amongst other operations, deals with medical evacuations and transportation of troops. Plus, there is the opportunity to meet some of the aircrew.

591 Signals Unit
A Cyber Protection Team parented by the Air Warfare Centre, 591SU

are responsible for safeguarding and supporting the global defence of military communications from enemy exploitation.

No 3 Mobile Catering Squadron
3 Mobile Catering Sqn is a highly deployable asset used in the support of Operations and Exercises worldwide...see the mobile field kitchen and how they cater for hundreds of personnel anywhere on the world stage.

RAF Regiment
The RAF Regiment is an elite fighting force trained to protect RAF personnel, bases and high-value assets. Since its formation in 1942, the Regiment and its 'Gunners' (as they are known) have seen action around the world. As a global fighting force, the RAF Regiment must be ready to serve anywhere in the world. Combat training is physically and mentally demanding and can take place in the jungles of Belize or the snow plains of the Arctic.

The Band of the Royal Air Force Regiment
Music has been a part of the Royal Air Force since 1912 - the primary role is to provide music for State and Service events. The Woodwind Quintet of the Band of the RAF Regiment consists of flute, oboe, clarinet, bassoon and French horn. Do have a chat with them if you would like to know any more about music in the Royal Air Force.

No1 Radio School
Number 1 Radio School is based at RAF Cosford and forms part of the Defence College of Communications and Information Systems.

The Red Arrows Support Team
The perfect opportunity for you to meet the Red Arrows groundcrew and support staff, known as "The Blues', and hopefully some of the pilots!

RAF Recruiting and Motivational Outreach Team
Want to find out more about a career in the Royal Air Force? Here's your chance, with members of the Air Force available to answer any questions and provide you with all the information you need.

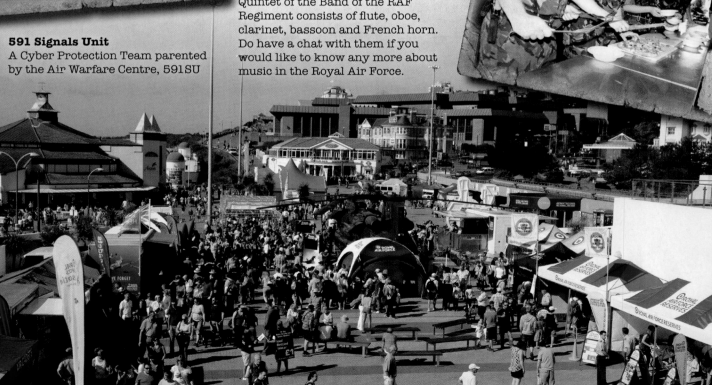

ROYAL AIR FORCE VILLAGE

Air Training Corps

Expand your horizons: If you're a fan of aviation, action, adventure, love sports and meeting people then you're in the right place.

Every year nearly 60,000 air cadets and volunteer staff take part in exciting events all over the country. Meet members of the Air Training Corps, a great place to start if you're interested in joining the youth organisation.

The Jon Egging Trust

Created in memory of Flight Lieutenant Jon Egging, The Jon Egging Trust inspires young people to take control of their lives and to be the best they can be, sharing with them his enthusiasm for flying and teamwork.

Hounds for Heroes Charity

Providing specially trained assistance dogs to injured and disabled service men and women of both the UK armed forces and civilian emergency services, Hounds for Heroes' gives help and practical support leading to an enhanced quality of life for their clients.

Royal Air Force Benevolent Fund

Since their foundation in 1919, the Royal Air Force Benevolent Fund supports RAF families including serving and former members as well as their partners and children.

Royal Air Force Association

A membership organisation and registered charity that provides welfare support to the RAF Family.

4624 Royal Auxiliary Air Force Squadron

Learn more about 4624 Squadron who shift vital items and supplies everywhere from exotic locations to hotspots. These include vital supplies for the army and humanitarian aid for flood victims – whatever is needed is both loaded and off-loaded by this squadron.

600 (City of London) Squadron Royal Auxiliary Air Force

600 Squadron is one of the oldest squadrons in the RAF Reserves. They provide specific training in five areas Personnel Support; Information Communications and Technology; Flight Operations; Intelligence; and Medical Support.

ROYAL AIR FORCE

PATRONS

The Official Air Festival Patrons 100 Club, now in its fifth year, continues to gain superb support from local businesses and aviation enthusiasts. Providing vital funding and considerable benefits to the Air Festival, this year's donations have funded the Red Devils Night Air display. Another great benefit of the Patrons scheme is that £10 from every membership fee is divided between the Air Festival charities, The Royal Navy & Royal Marines Charity, The Not Forgotten Association, The British Lung Foundation and The Jon Egging Trust. A massive thank you to the members of the Patrons 100 Club for their donations and support for this year's Air Festival.

Abbey Life Assurance Company
A Bowring
Adam Greenwood, IA Digital
AMICA
Beach Weddings Bournemouth
Below Decks Custom Boat Carpets
Best Western Montague Hotel
BH Live
BoConcept Bournemouth
Bourne Engraving
Bournemouth Accommodation & Hotel Association (BAHA)
Bournemouth Airport
Bournemouth Aviation Museum
Bournemouth Barbecue Hire
Bournemouth Chamber of Trade and Commerce
Bournemouth Highcliff Marriott Hotel
Bournemouth Pier
Bournemouth Red Arrows Association
Bournemouth University
Cafe Riva
Campbell Rowley
Castle Cameras

Charles & Julia Millar
City Fibre
Councillor Christopher Rochester
Cumberland Hotel
DAL Strategy Limited
Deep South Media Limited
Discover Dorset Tours
Dorset Plane Pull
Dr Jonathan Menton – Portchester Dental Practice
East Cliff and Springbourne Ward Councillors – Councillor Anne Filer, Councillor Michael Filer and Councillor David Kelsey
Electric Beach Tanning Salon
FJB Hotels
Foresolutions
George Fry Limited
Glyn Electrical
Greendale Construction Limited
Head and Wheble Funeral Directors
High Flying Talks
Horsey Lightly Fynn
Hotel Miramar

Intrinity Business Events
John Thornton Young Achievers Foundation
Kiteleys Solicitors
Lester Aldridge
Menzies East Cliff Court and Carlton Hotels
Meridian Lifts
Merley House
Morgan Sindall
Mouchel
Mr Jody Ivie – Entrepreneur
Mrs Enid Thomas
Natwest Commercial Banking
Pat Dean
Plato Video
Princecroftwillis LLP
Quantum Recruitment
Queens Park Ward Councillors – Councillor Mark Anderson, Councillor Carol Ainge and Councillor Cheryl Johnson
Rotary Club of Parley
Roz Scammell, Strategic Liaison

Saffery Champness
Sembcorp Bournemouth Water
Spinners Carpet Cleaning
Stephen Young Lord of Westbury & Waxham
The Consultancy, Advertising, Marketing and PR
The Cottonwood Boutique & Ocean View Hotels
The Jon Egging Trust
The Metcalfe Partnership Professional Inventory Services
Urban Reef
Vulcan to the Sky, Team Bournemouth
Westbourne and West Cliff Ward Councillors – Councillor John Beesley – Leader of the Council, Councillor Barry Goldbart and Councillor Rae Stollard
West Southbourne Ward Councillors – Councillor Allister Russell, Councillor Blair Crawford, Councillor Chris Mayne, The Mayor
Whitehall and Arlington Hotels
White House Group

For details and to become a member of the 2015 Patrons 100 Club visit bournemouthair.co.uk

TRADE STANDS
With 1.5 miles of trading space between the Piers and along the East Overcliff here's your complete list to who's on the ground...

Access Point Ltd. (Solar Fusion)
Aden Veteran's Association
Adlems - Red Arrows Merch
AECC - Chiropractic College and Clinics
All Out Leisure
Andrews Leisure
Army- Regular & Reserve
Atlanta Beads
Avon Cosmetics
Barny
Battersea Dogs and Cats Home
BH Live
Blue Harbour Catering Ltd
Bon Voyage Travel & Tours – USA experts
Bournemouth Airport
Bournemouth Leathercraft
Bournemouth Merchandise
Bournemouth Round Table
Bournemouth Veterans & Friends Association
Bournemouth YMCA
C&P Dinner Jackets
Campbell Rowley
Casa Carlos Cafe - Tuckton
Churros Garcia
City Fibre
Coffee Cab
Combat Stress
Costco Wholesale
Daily Echo

D&S Sweets
Dills Catering
Dorset Fire & Rescue
Dorset Wildlife Trust
Dreamroof Ltd
DRG Trading
Eat Fresh Catering
Elms Event Catering
Explore Learning
Falconry UK
Flavastation
Foster Care Associates (FCA)
Four Legged Fancies
"Free From" Healthy Alternative Tour
Freemasonry in the Community
Giggi Gelateria
Gourmet Farm
Green Goals
Haribo
Help for Heroes - Kilimanjaro Trek 2015
Hi Therapies Ltd
Hop on Inn
Ignite Solutions Ltd (in assoc with Now TV)
Inspired Toys and Games
Iris Imports
Just-Imagine Glitter Tattoos
K L Perfumes
Kai's Candies & Sweets
Kayu Kraft
Lancaster Bomber

Limelight Garments
Littledown
Maritime Volunteer Service - Poole Unit
Multiply UK Ltd
My Mum's Cakes etc
National Trust
Nintendo
NowTV / Ignite Solutions Ltd
O'Hagan's Sausage BBQ & Spit Roast Co.
Peppercoast Ltd
Perfect World
Personalised Gifts
Personalised Ragdolls
Pieroth Wines
Piggin Lush Hog Roast Co Ltd
Poole Flying Boats Celebration
Posh Nosh Catering
Prestige Holiday Homes
Radio Solent
RFU/The Rugby Store
RNLI
Road Safety Team – Bournemouth Borough Council
Rob's Event Catering
Rose's of Bournemouth
Royal Air Force
Royal Navy & Marines Recruiting
RSPB Dorset
Samsung UHD Discovery Lounge
Shorefield Holidays

Simply Strawberries
Solar Fusion
Stedmans Catering
SSAFA Dorset - Lifelong Support for our Forces and their Families
SWWFL - Dorset Wildlife Trust
S&D Simulations Ltd
Tanks Heroes – Mini Tanks
Thaiangle
Thai Smile Restaurant
The Ashai Koh Lounge
The National Museum of the Royal Navy
The Poppy Shop
The Royal British Legion Trading Ltd
The Royal Naval Association
Thomas Cook
Three Cross Motorcycles Ltd
Transformers Optimus Prime Truck Tour
UK Homes 4 Heroes Pride & Passion
Vicomte Bernard De Romanet Ltd
Vulcan to the Sky
Waterfront Fish Bar
Westbeach
Wicked Coatings
www.littletikes.co.uk
Working 4 Wildlife (RSPB)
Yums Yums

Riverside Court –
Now open & ready to make your own

Riverside Court
TUCKTON PLACE

An exclusive development by:
MansellHomes

- 1 & 2 bedroom luxury retirement apartments
- Estate Manager
- Gated Parking

- Owners' lounge
- Guest Suite
- Lift to all floors
- High specification

Prices from £224,995

Open everyday
10am – 4pm
Call **01202 429653**

Prices correct at time of going to press. Computer Generated Image depicts apartments at Riverside Court, Tuckton Place. Photography depicts the residential lounge, typical kitchen & bathroom at Riverside Court.

riversidecourt@stubbingsltd.co.uk
www.tucktonplace.co.uk

Mansell Homes are proud sponsors of Air Festival TV

A **Balfour Beatty** Company

THANKS

**The Bournemouth Tourism Management Board
would like to thank the following groups for their help
in the organisation of the 2014 Bournemouth Air Festival...**

- Air Festival Media: Wave 105, Daily Echo and BBC Radio Solent
- Air Festival Patrons
- Air Festival Patrons Venues:
  Bournemouth Highcliff Marriott
  Menzies Hotel
  Queen's Hotel
  The Chine Hotel
  The Cottonwood Boutique Hotel
  The Cumberland Hotel
- Air Festival Sponsors
- Armed Forces: Royal Navy, Royal Marines, Royal Air Force and The Army
- BHLive Trust
- Bournemouth Air Festival Ground and Site Group
- Bournemouth Air Festival Marketing and Content Group
- Bournemouth Air Festival Medical Group
- Bournemouth Air Festival Safety Advisory Group
- Bournemouth Air Festival Steering Group
- Bournemouth Air Festival Traffic Management Group
- Bournemouth Airport
- Bournemouth Aviation Museum
- Bournemouth Borough Council
- Bournemouth Tourism
- Bournemouth Town Centre BID
- Bournemouth Coastal BID
- Campbell Rowley
- Local Coastal Ward Councillors
- Debbie Sadd
- DS Aviation and Julian Jones
- Emergency Services: Dorset Police, HM Coastguard, RNLI Lifeguards,
  South Western Ambulance Service Trust, Dorset Fire and Rescue and Red Cross
- Festival Maker Volunteers
- Global Aviation Resources
- David Bailey from Hotel Miramar
- John Green from Hot Rocks
- Maritime Volunteer Service
- Paul Johnson Flightline UK
- Poole Harbour Commissioners
- TSA Consulting (Air Display Management)

- Designed by: Neil Keeping
- Written by: Steven Smith (Daily Echo) and the
Bournemouth Tourism team

- To Advertise in next years programme: Tracy Hayden,
Daily Echo Advertisement Sales Manager 01202 411225
- Contributing Photographers: Darren Harbar, Jamie Hunter,
John Higgins, Karl Drage, Paul Johnson, Daily Echo Staff
Photographers and Rob Fleming.

DAILY ECHO

Published by the Daily Echo Bournemouth
Newsquest Dorset, Richmond Hill, Bournemouth, BH2 6HH
Tel: Main Switchboard: 01202 554601
bournemouthecho.co.uk

Printed by: Acorn Web Offset LTD, acornweb.co.uk